Sergio Magaña (Ocelocoyotl)

2012-2021:
the Dawn of the Sixth Sun

The Path of Quetzalcoatl

Foreword by Elizabeth B. Jenkins

Translated by Stefano Cozzi
Art cover by Amritagraphic

GW00676306

blossomjngbooks

First published 2012 by
Blossoming Books:
www.blossomingbooks.com

Blossoming Books is a trademark of Edizioni Amrita srl

Edizioni Amrita srl
Via San Quintino, 36
10121 Torino - Italy
www.amrita-edizioni.com

Printed in United States of America

both collectively and individually, as the Age of the Sixth Sun unfolds. This book is an instruction manual for anyone who wants to awaken from the dream-like trance of ordinary reality and attain a truly lucid state."

~ Daniel Pinchbeck,
Executive Director of Evolver.net
and author of 2012: TheReturn of Quetzalcoatl

"2012 – 2021: The Dawn of the Sixth Sun - The Path of Quetzalcoatl shows us that the knowledge and tradition of the pre-Colombian people of Mesoamerica, creators of the Mayan and Aztec calendars, has not been lost. They speak to us now at this critical time in history and generously give us practices and insight based on their understanding of cosmic mathematics. The ancient knowledge that Sergio Magaña shares in this book teaches us how to realign ourselves with the universe so that we can play our true role as conduits for the transition from one era of human consciousness to the next."

~ Dr. Marilyn Schlitz,
Global Ambassador and Senior Scientist,
Institute of Noetic Sciences

"This is not a book to read. This is a book to study. Take it seriously! Sergio is not alone in saying these things, although the language may be unfamiliar. In essence he says, 'Clean up your act now—don't delay!' Other traditions have been saying this in a much more muted way—i.e. Buddhist teachers etc. I am looking forward to trying the exercises."

~ Gay Luce,
Founder of Nine Gates Mystery School

CONTENTS

Everybody wants to change the world,
but nobody thinks of changing himself.
Leo Tolstoy

Our human urge toward wholeness has propelled a rash of publications over the past sixty years, weaving together Eastern and Western philosophies and spiritualities in the studies of human consciousness. These past thirty years have seen the emergence of the precious wisdoms of the South, Central America and of course, Mexico. The real work of integration is only now just beginning. Each culture holds a choice and tasty morsel of our spiritual wholeness, however not all books provide an equally nutritious meal. I am delighted to write the foreword for this wonderful new addition primarily because it afforded me the pleasure and honor of reading it. There could not be a more timely or important book.

Quite simply, this book is a masterpiece. Sergio Magaña has managed the nigh impossible task of translating not only a little-known authentic oral tradition of the Mexica people, but their profound and complex cosmology as well. The information contained in these pages offers a glorious vista into indigenous science; a human-yet-mathematical worldview based in the precision of the cycles of Great Nature. This knowledge coupled with the direct means to personally engage these cycles, provides the reader the exact spiritual food required at this time. In the writing of this book Sergio has opened a window into the reality of a wise and sacred people who have come through time to save us now, at the turning of the tide.

Dawn of the Sixth Sun is written with the original Nahuatl language intact in its pages. While this is something publishers generally find troublesome, it is absolutely essential to the honoring and bringing forth of this genuine Mexica tradition. Great power is held in the vibration of ancient language, and Sergio has done an impeccable job giving us just enough Nahuatl to taste and try wrapping our tongues around, while defining in clear and concise language the meaning of these 'hard to translate' words and transmitting to us the fabulous cosmovision they spring from.

Sergio delivers well-guarded oral prophecies from ancient wisdom keepers that define our time, explaining the meaning of the 'Suns' 1-5, and setting the stage for what is coming (6th Sun), with us as the main players. Next there is—at long last—a coherent explanation of the Aztec and Mayan calendar system and those 'Castanedian' terms 'tonal,' 'nahual,' and 'dreaming while awake.' Sergio then takes us by the hand, step by step into a world of 13 heavens and down through 9 underworlds, building a foundation of knowledge that shows us the meaning and importance of each layer of reality and how they fit together in a cycle of constant creation that is both personal and cosmic. Based on the cosmological framework he has provided, Sergio can then deliver the nectar of the tradition—actual practices to cleanse the shadow, engage the power of the cosmic forces, and step like a warrior into life, dreaming, and death.

What sets this book apart from the crowd is the authenticity of knowledge and depth of framework Sergio provides in order to offer practices that are clearly stated, easy to use and yet exceedingly powerful. The fact that this knowledge is NOT available elsewhere, as it comes directly from oral traditions, makes this book all the more challenging to write and all the more precious to hold in our hands. Let this serve as a warning to those who think they are 'just reading' a book. Engage in these practices and YOUR LIFE WILL CHANGE!   ⁕

My work of the last 25 years within the Inka tradition has elaborated meaning in our human/nature relationships, providing an organic framework of human spiritual development, while focusing on the use of living energy within our intentional and conscious life; an apt expertise for those known as 'the children of the sun.'

The techniques offered here target in great detail the essential work of the Moon: the acknowledgement and cleansing of the shadow, and the process of intentional dreaming; the Mexica approach to the unconscious. I find these techniques a powerful complement to those of their more Southerly Inka cousins.

Now, I want to take a moment in this foreword to give you readers the honor that I have had, of getting to know this author personally. I first met Sergio in the fall of 2008 when he attended a seminar at my farm in Hawaii. Sergio, while a charmingly perfect gentleman, was quite shy and retiring, telling us no more about himself than "I have a radio show in Mexico." It was only later the following year, after he invited me to teach in Mexico City, that I discovered the fantastic healing center he had founded, the scope and range of Sergio's abilities as a healer, and the extent of his well-deserved fame in Mexico. He never spoke about any of his accomplishments until I questioned him, and then, only under duress. Like most authentic healers, teachers, and real 'persons of power,' Sergio is a bit of a reluctant messenger; the honest stance of someone with a true calling as a 'cultural bridge,' due to the enormous responsibilities involved. Since his naming ceremony described at the beginning of this book, he has stepped resolutely onto the path. This however, does not make it an easy one. Ocelocoyotl I salute your daring, your loyalty, your bravery, your commitment!

I continue to be profoundly grateful to Sergio as his invitation to Mexico afforded me several pivotal experiences of perception that have changed my life. Upon first setting foot on the motherland of Mexico City I found myself instantly bombarded, deluged, crushed to near drowning by the thunderous waves of power rolling over me, emanating from the sacred central geography that is Tenochtitlan, central Mexico City. Second, I became captivated by the immediate knowledge of the crucial role this sacred power center has to play in the flowering forth of the new human culture that we are currently unfolding. My previous 25 years found me working steadily at the NAVEL of this unfoldment, in Cuzco, Peru. In coming to Mexico City, I found I had at last arrived to its HEART.

I can think of nothing more beautiful than to be in accurate, artistic, and intentional harmony with the glory of our sacred cosmos. Sergio offers us that incomparable gift in sharing with us these ancient techniques, to do just what our souls yearn for. To belong. To be connected. To become intentionally one with the cycles and rhythms of what is happening right now on our earth. To participate in this dramatic moment of historic change as the human part of the planetary body begins to perceive itself as one being. What could be more exciting? Why else would we choose to be born here…now…if not to take part in this great turning of the wheel? Why else would you be reading this right now!

Bravo Sergio for a stunning job beyond well done. Bravo Amrita/BlossomingBooks for recognizing the importance, beauty, and power of this tradition and publishing the book as you have. I repeat: THIS BOOK IS A MASTERPIECE.

I, for one, shall use the practices and knowledge herein diligently to ready myself so that we may together become the Dawn of the Sixth Sun, paving the road with flowers, chants and dances that Quetzalcoatl, the Sapa Inka, Sapa Qoya and all sacred beings of all traditions may walk united on this earth in love and power. May Mexico in each of us flower forth to accomplish her sacred and magnificent, lush and fragrant destiny. OMETEOTL!

Elizabeth B. Jenkins
Hawaii, February 14, 2012

How did it all Start? The Sowing of the Name

> "*Ni ye Ocelocoyotl*   "I am Ocelocoyotl,
> *yah yac*   force and power.
> *yah xac*"   I am a spring, and I emanate"

This greeting in the Nahuatl language contains words of power. My original name is Sergio Magaña, and since my youth I have been following a number of spiritual paths and have developed a number of healing techniques, which have turned out to be incredibly effective for thousands of people both in Mexico, my native country, and in other countries too, and which I have since shared with my students.

One day, a great Andean master told me something very beautiful, and later in my life he was proved totally right: "Although you may begin your spiritual awakening by following some other path, the one that is actually calling you is the voice of your land and tradition." I therefore heeded my calling: I went to the sacred mountains of Mexico, Popocatapetl and Iztaccihuatl, where I made offerings based on the little knowledge that I had at the time of making offerings; there I requested permission to gain the knowledge of my own land and asked that the masters would come to me.

And so it happened. I came across my first master without searching for him: he appeared as one of my students, and it was only afterwards that he started to teach me. Thank you, Hugo, for your far-reaching vision! You recognised my path well before I did... and the others too appeared in the same way. After deepening my studies, I decided to step resolutely into this tradition, through 'the sowing of the name'.

It is only Mother Earth who can give us a Nahuatl name, and this name is based upon the influences present at birth and what is indicated in the calendar. This is how we are introduced to all the energies, or 'essences'–as we call them–of ancient Mexico, and to the community as well, so that they are able to recognise us by our new name. It is like a new birth and a new destiny, which is why I shall no longer refer to anything I did before this day, as it was at this juncture that my new life commenced.

On 21 December 2010 various cosmic influences manifested simultaneously: the winter solstice, a full moon and an eclipse, and for we followers of the *Mexihcahyotl*[1] it was also the celebration of the birth of *Huitzilopochtli*, the 'hummingbird that flies to the left', which through its messages in the lucid dreaming state would guide the Mexicas (*Mexihcah* in the Nahuatl language) to become the greatest empire across the whole of ancient Mexico. Huitzilopochtli, to whom I have dedicated Chapter 11, is the energy that rules the Southern direction in the waking state world; it is this energy that removes all thorny obstacles from the path, and bestows the strength to persevere and bring all projects to fruition.

For me, however, this day was even more special: it represented the culmination of my constant quest for the knowledge of ancient Mexico. My master Xolotl[2] sowed a Nahuatl name in me, and presented me to the energies and the cardinal points[3].

1 The pre-Hispanic tradition of Mexico, which corresponds to Aztecs and Toltecs.

2 Xolotl is one of the main keepers of the Mexihcahyotl: he lives in Mexico City and has been travelling around the Nahuatl-speaking communities of Mexico for about 30 years. The Nahuatl is the ancient pre-Hispanic language, which is still spoken by almost 1.5 million people, and he has therefore salvaged this ancient knowledge. He now teaches Nahuatl language and culture, as well as ancient warrior dances and sacred Mexihcahyotl philosophy.

3 The cardinal points are where the different energies are located. East, or *Tlauhcopa*, is the direction of the Sun, of the willpower of male warriors, and of knowledge; North, or *Mictlampa*, is the direction of death, where our ancestors and the world of dreaming reside; West, or *Cihuatlampa*, is the

I therefore received new responsibilities and a new name that I had to honour, *Ocelocoyotl* (coyote jaguar), given to me by *Tonantzin Coatlicue*, the ancient Mother Earth of Mexico City, whose old name was *Tenochtitlan*[4].

That day I asked that all thorny obstacles to the spread of the truth of the ancient knowledge of this land be removed, and I asked to acquire the necessary willpower to accomplish such a task; from that moment on two mixed energies started to coexist inside me, as it says in the prophecy: "melted metal in clay pots". My parents, who attended the ceremony, presented me with a gift, a very ancient book that my mother had obtained from her father, who was of Spanish descent: *The True History of the Conquest of New Spain* by Bernal Diaz Del Castillo.

Inside the book my mother wrote a dedication that deeply moved me, and which further clarified the very purpose of my life, of my history and quest, and it is this that I now wish to share with all my readers, because it contains the essence of the book that you are holding in your hands:

"Sergio Ocelocoyotl, you are the blend of two races.

Today we present you with this book, which we have guarded for many years: we put into your hands one of the two parts of which you are made. The other, which represents the true history of our ancestors, our forefathers of the great

direction of fertility, where female warriors reside, that is all those women who, as true heroines, have died giving birth to their children, as well as the enlightened women we speak of in Chapter 13; South, or *Huitztlampa*, is the direction of the Hummingbird, which represents the determination to overcome all difficulties, as well as the universe of lucid dreaming. The South is also the direction of *Tlalocan*, the Heaven of the Four Waters, see Chapter 13, 'Tlaloc Quetzalcoatl', page 135.

4 In our tradition, the physical Earth, which belongs to the waking state or *tonal*, is called *Tonantzin*, meaning 'our venerable Mother'. Like every mother, she is given the task of naming her children, which she does by using a *tlamacazqui*, or 'he who looks after the essences' (or energies), as the channel or vehicle; although there is only one Tonantzin, she is traditionally named after the place in which we find ourselves: our tradition in fact acknowledges her as possessing different qualities or energies which vary according to different locations.

Mesoamerican culture, that part shall be your task to write, together with others, truthfully, with pride and with passion, so that it becomes known in every corner of the world.

Be proud to be the outcome of this blend: you are part of the so-called 'cosmic race' that shall shine like the sun over our land of Anáhuac.[5]

May today mark the start of a new life for you.

Your parents, 21 December 2010".

These words remained etched in my spirit: to write truthfully, with pride and with passion, one part of that ancient knowledge which belongs to this land so sacred to me. In this book you will not come across a single word stemming from official or academic sources of knowledge, instead you will find the spoken word, the 'flowers and chants' of the guardians of the Toltec and Mexica traditions, which they handed down from father to son, from master to disciple, according to Cuauhtémoc's prophecy (see Chapter 2, 'The Prophecy'): this knowledge is profound poetry, the practice of the sacred oral tradition called *mah toteotahtzin mitsmopieli*, 'the tale of our Venerable Land'.

My mother's writing was pointing to something that had been prophesized to me by my master Hugo Nahui some five years earlier. He said to me that his own master Esteban had in turn prophesized that the Mexica wisdom would spread across the world following the eclipse of 11 July 2010, and that teachers from our tradition would go and teach in Europe, starting from Italy, as that was ...as that was Columbus' birthplace and the seat of Catholicism.

The type of order that had been established in the Americas at the time of the conquistadors (the conquerors) and which resulted in so much suffering and destruction, had in a sense originated from there. The conquistadors, not to mention the rest of Europe in those days, were not prepared to listen to our ancient wisdom, so the next available opportunity for momentous change–which is actually available right now–ought to start

5 This is the Nahuatl name of the entire land that stretches from Alaska down to Nicaragua.

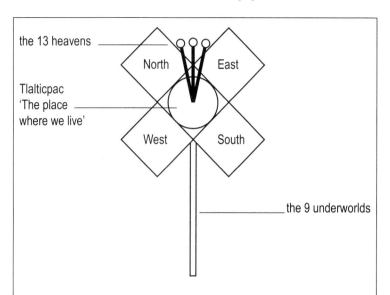

the 13 heavens

North   East

Tlalticpac
'The place
where we live'

West   South

the 9 underworlds

'Flowers and chants' is a traditional way to refer to the entire creation. The place where we live is described as the centre of a flower, whose petals are the 4 cardinal points and whose pistils are the 13 heavens, while the stalk represents the 9 underworlds: the Mexica universe was therefore a flower and this is why the term which corresponds to enlightenment in our tradition is 'flowering', or 'blossoming'. We must actualize this flower and transform its potential into an actual flower; we must transform ourselves into the beauty of the blossoming flower, as by definition flowers represent beauty. We therefore become this flower, and the flower is the universe, and thus we become the universe. This is shown by the 'Lord of the flowers', one of the epithets, or names, of Quetzalcoatl, as depicted in the cover.

from there as well, and would constitute the opportunity to heal that past. Hugo told me that I would be one of those teachers, and I did not believe him at all: it was not something I was looking to achieve in my life, so I just kept practising our tradition for my own benefit and the benefit of my students in Mexico.

But in May 2010 I received an invitation to go to Hawaii to give a lecture on healing at a conference on Andean traditions, and it was actually there that this prophecy, which in turn is based on more ancient ones, as you will read in the next chapter, started to unfold and provoked a huge change in my life. It was at this conference that I started to receive invitations to teach in other parts of the world, and especially–and quite unexpectedly–in Italy, just as Hugo had foreseen.

The purpose of this book is to reveal for the first time this oral tradition by showing its authenticity, and thus put an end to many distorted interpretations: it will first appear, oddly enough, not in Mexico and in the Spanish language, but in Italy and in Italian! Only afterwards, with the coming of the Sixth Sun,[6] will it be published in other countries, in their respective languages.

2012 is a date engraved both in the *tzolkin*, the Mayan calendar, which everyone is now familiar with, and in the *cuauhxicalli*, the lesser-known Toltec-Mexica calendar: both calendars were created in Mexico, but the majority of people who wrote about them only had partial access to this tradition, or decided to add their own interpretation. Often, therefore, what they wrote would significantly differ from the oral transmission of the guardians of the tradition, my Mexica masters Xolotl and Hugo Nahui, and as such you will be amazed at the differences between the contents of this book and others that you may already be familiar with.

I personally feel like a bridge that links the ancient Mexica culture with its modern counterpart, given that both are part of my blood, and the latter is represented by my Spanish heritage. My deepest aspiration in writing this book is to establish an authentic bridge so that you too can taste this ancient Mexica wisdom: as the prophecy says, this wisdom must be disseminated right now, so that we all can understand what is going on at this crucial time, in this transition from the Fifth to the Sixth Sun, when according to this ancient training we must transform ourselves into our *Quetzalcoatl*.

Is this going to be the end of the world? Or will it be the end of *one* world?

What is the real meaning of this passage from the Fifth to the Sixth Sun, and how can we prepare for it? What will be the consequences of either acting, or of not acting?

---

6 According to the Toltec-Aztec-Mexica calendar, a 'Sun' is an astronomical period lasting 6,625 years, which is part of a larger cycle of 26,500 years, corresponding to the passage of our Sun around Alcyone, the central sun of the Pleiades. Currently we are in a period of transition between the previous sun, the Fifth, and the Sixth.

I would hereby like to pay a special tribute to all my masters, Xolotl, Hugo Nahui and others like Xochicuauhtli, who gave me some extraordinary initiations, and to many others who have deeply touched my life with their wisdom, including those who do not wish to be named. I also wish to pay tribute to their own masters, in this vast lineage of teachers and teachings. They are the true authors of this book, and I pray to all the masters who reside in the *Mictlan*, the 'place of the dead', to support me in this task of sharing–most authentically and to the best of my abilities–the ancient wisdom of Anáhuac, so that it may blossom again in all its beauty and perfection in those who wish to follow it and put it into practice. They will become their own Quetzalcoatl, a term that possesses several meanings, but that in this context specifically signifies 'the precious energy that has blossomed'.

Ometeotl![7]

---

7 This is a traditional expression, which means 'may this become real' or, more literally, 'the two energies [may combine to create]', as depicted by a double-headed serpent. It also means 'the union of the energy heavens and of the physical world'.

2 (OME)

The Prophecy

*"Let us leave behind chants, flowers and dances,
so that the world of Anáhuac may continue to exist at this time"
(Cuauhtémoc's Legacy)*

The oral chronicles recount that seven tribes set off from Aztlan–which for some people represents a mythical land but for others is a real place–in search of a promised land. Aztlan is described as a land dotted with white houses, inhabited by many herons and where the locals–all good and wise people–spoke the Nahuatl language: the name 'Aztec' actually originates from here.

Three councils ruled the weakest of all the Aztec groups, which was controlled by the other six tribes: one council was formed by wise male elders, one by warriors, and one by women; they would debate and take decisions and the *tlahtoani*, 'the bearer of the word', was their social and spiritual leader. The tlahtoani was the spokesperson who communicated the decisions taken by the members of the three councils to the rest of the tribe: he performed a communicative rather than a governing function, for instance relaying army orders, something that the three councils were not entitled to do. The tlahtoani and the council of wise elders received some messages in a dream from the hummingbird (*huitzilin* in Nahuatl), who was the *nahual* of the group ('nahual' means a powerful animal that appears in lucid dreams to guide our consciousness); in this case the instructions stated that they must separate from the rest of the Aztec tribes.

A few days later, while they were eating, the elders noticed a hummingbird that came to rest on top of a tree, which then split into two, and they took this as a prophetic sign of their separation and independence. The hummingbird signalled to them– both in their dreams and in the state of dreaming while awake, a kind of trance–that they had to let go of the name *Aztec*, which comes from Aztlan, and change it to *Mexihcah* (currently Mexica), the 'location of the navel of the Moon': the Moon in fact governs the knowledge of dreams, a knowledge whose mastery the Mexicas would develop in an unrivalled fashion across the whole of the ancient world.

The hummingbird taught them how to use their willpower to overcome their weaknesses, and pointed out to them the land where they ought to settle down: they would recognise it from a *nopal* (a cactus), on top of which they would see an eagle devour a snake. After travelling for a long time and experiencing a great deal of suffering in the process, while following the guide of the hummingbird in their lucid dreaming or in the state of dreaming while awake, the Mexicas came across the abovementioned signs on an islet, which is where they founded their city, Tenochtitlan, which is known today as Mexico City.

They freed themselves from the yoke of their neighbouring tribes and managed to conquer them all; they then created the Aztec empire, which was so named because it included the other tribes that hailed from Aztlan. The Mexica culture reached the highest peaks both in the arts and in astronomy (as expressed by their calendars), as well as the highest form of knowledge and spirituality of ancient Mexico.

Keen to express their gratitude to the hummingbird for guiding them in the dream state as far as their promised land and to their greatest expansion, they made it their principal deity, *Huitzilopochtli*, 'the hummingbird that flies to the left', the warrior who is equipped with both discipline and willpower.

They named this land *Anáhuac*, which in Nahuatl means 'in between the waters', and its territory stretched all the way from Alaska to Nicaragua; the name *Nican Anáhuac*, or 'here is Anáhuac', comes from the Nahuatl language, just like a myriad of other names across the American continent.

All these lands now await in silence the new awakening of the sounds of the culture that gave them their name in a far-off past, as well as the blossoming of that knowledge which ruled for thousands of years prior to the arrival of the Spanish conquerors. According to the oral tradition, when Cortez appeared with his army of less than a hundred men, the tlahtoani ('the bearer of the word') Motecuhzoma, a real master of prophetic dreams, saw that the 'barbarians' would come, take his land and break the balance between man and nature, and then multiply in order to have enough people to withstand the transition from the Fifth to the Sixth Sun, which is the one happening at present. In light of this, Motecuhzoma decided to give them what they wanted without putting up a fight, but Cuitlahuac, the next in line to the tlahtoani, who did not possess the same mastery of dreams as his uncle Motecuhzoma, did not want to surrender, hence he killed him and ordered the attack. Only one single battle took place against the Spaniards and their allies (namely neighbouring tribes, which had been subjugated by the Mexicas), the 'Battle of the Night of Sorrows', where the Spaniards were totally defeated. Their bodies fell into the lagoon that surrounded Tenochtitlan. As many of them had contracted smallpox, this could be regarded as the first ever example of biological warfare: when the Mexica army, after defeating the Spaniards, went to wash in the lagoon, they all fell ill, including Cuitlahuac, who was the first to die. This is the origin of the legend of *Llorona*, the 'wailing one', the dead woman who shouts: "My poor children!", who were actually killed by her; for many, however, it evokes the voice of the lagoon, lamenting the death of its own children, which it had caused.

The next tlahtoani, Cuauhtémoc, saw therefore that Motecuhzoma had been right all along, and that everything was unfolding according to the prophecy: he realized that he did not have enough time to assemble a new army before the return of the Spaniards, and so there was absolutely nothing that he could do.

With his few remaining men and many women and children, he managed to hide all their treasures, thus avoiding their total destruction, and although the Spaniards kept searching for Cuauhtémoc's treasure throughout the ensuing three hundred years, to this day most of it still remains undiscovered.

According to our oral tradition, the Spaniards surrounded Tenochtitlan, which by now was only defended by women and children, and on 12 August 1521 Cuauhtémoc, the last great tlahtoani, made a speech in front of the entire Mexica population, which represents his bequest to posterity and is famously known as *Cuauhtémoc's Legacy*. The people gathered there had come from every corner of the empire: they all listened very attentively and carefully memorized his speech so that it could be spread to each of the four directions of the Nahuatl-speaking world. It was actually handed down orally from generation to generation and carefully guarded by the custodians of ancient Mexico, and even today a whole host of guardians continue to disseminate this oral tradition in an effort to prevent it from dying out, and to ensure that it lives on in our memory. Six versions of it still exist and they all preserve the same essence, albeit with some minor variations.

The Legacy has been carved in stone and can be currently found in El Zócalo, the main square in Mexico City, the location of the remnants of the Templo Mayor, the main Mexica temple, which equally silently awaits the resurgence of this wisdom and extraordinary knowledge which, according to the prophecy, shall blossom and come back to light with the advent of the Sixth Sun.

Now the time has come and the ancient prophecy is being fulfilled: the hummingbird and its messages are flying again and they will spread and reveal Cuauhtémoc's Legacy and the ancient Mexica wisdom to the entire world.

Cuauhtémoc's Legacy,
the Historic Directive of the Young Tlahtoani Cuauhtémoc

"Our Sun has hidden itself behind daggers made of obsidian.[8]
Sad evening for Anáhuac, for the Texcoco[9] *and for Mexihco-Tenochtitlan.*
Tonatiuh [the sun] *is painting the sky with blood: silence, oblivion and bitter tears.*
Tonalli [the day] *follows its path and leaves us in the total*

---

8 Obsidian is a very dark black volcanic rock, which the Mexicas used to make weapons and mirrors; in this context it is a type of knife.
9 A population allied with the Mexicas.

darkness of Yohualli [the night].

To die on this earth for the blossomed war.[10]

The shadows of the night descend.

The moon and the stars are the winners of the cosmic battle, in their fight against the light of the day.

Abysses of destiny, the life of beings in labyrinths of inescapable mystery.

Let us all go and leave the streets deserted, disappearing from the marketplaces and from their paths.

Let us lock ourselves up in our houses, turning our eternal ideals into fortresses, lost in this deep solitude, in a pointless dialogue inside this great void.

Let us preserve in our hearts the wisdom and love contained in the códices [the scriptures],[11] *the* teocalli [the temples], *the* tepochcalli [pelota courts],[12] *the* cuicacalli [buildings for dancing, singing and the arts],

until the Sixth Sun appears again, from the bosom of our future women.

Mother Tonantzin Iztaccíhuatl,[13] *asleep today with white mantles and green forests, shall awaken tomorrow between thunderclaps and redeeming lightnings of authentic freedom.*

---

10 This expression means 'dying as a warrior' and was also used to refer to a debate in which one contestant, equipped with knowledge, would gain the upper hand and all would acknowledge that his knowledge had "blossomed the most".

11 The remains of these ancient códices, or scriptures, are named after whoever discovered or preserved them, as in the case of the Borgia Codex. Most of them are housed in the Vatican or in other private collections, both in Europe and in the United States. Copies of these códices can be viewed and are made available to whoever wishes to study them but, according to the oral tradition, the most important–and there are quite a few of them–remain hidden; several are said to be buried under the cathedral in Mexico City, and Mother Earth Tonantzin shall reveal them when the people are ready to receive and understand such wisdom, at which point an earthquake shall unearth them.

12 The game of *pelota*, played with a kind of rubber ball, was actually not a game at all: it was a form of training for the best warriors, where one of them symbolized the light and the other the darkness, and the whole game was a sort of oracular prediction of the movements of the universe, aimed at anticipating events and take decisions accordingly.

13 An extinct Mexican volcano, located just in front of and joined with the better-known Popocatepetl: it is considered a sacred and feminine mountain.

*She will resurrect amidst whirlwinds, emotional currents
and burning flames of light.*

*The mother country that was once burnt shall shine with the
new Sun that will save Mexico.*

*She will be born from the blood spilt across green lands and
white cotton fields; the hope in the One Life shall shine, far
beyond our temporal death.*

*Once our great history will have been severed, we know that
the extension of the* centli *corn* [one corn][14] *shall manifest
again to light up our forehead;*

*then Cuauhtémoc, the solar eagle, shall rise up and the spirit
of the eagle-warriors*[15] *shall rule again and govern Anáhuac.*

The will of Huitzilopochtli [the hummingbird] *shall be born
amongst the warriors of the discipline.*

The tlamatinime *masters* [the wise men] *will have different
faces, more truthful and stronger.*

*They will come with the flaming voice of the conch, the spi-
ral of the flowered snake.*

Today those chants and dances that hold no hope for triumph
are abandoned in exhaustion.

*The time tolls for the dreadful omen of the supreme secret to
occur already and, last messenger of the sacred solar tradition of Tollán the Ancient,*[16]

the Great Sage Ce Acatl Topiltzin Quetzalcoatl,[17]

*the visionary, who hurled to the four winds prophetic words
containing future images: wild, beast-like barbarians will*

---

14 The One energy, the One god, represented by 'the mathematics' of the corn.
15 The Mexica culture comprised three major trainings: the eagle, the jaguar
and the snake trainings. These had both a military and a spiritual nature, as
is the case in some Eastern traditions: the Eagle warriors specialized in the
Tonal, the waking state, and in the power of the Sun; the Jaguars were great
specialists of the *Nahual*, the dream state, and of the forces of the Night,
while the Snake warriors worked with the elemental forces of the Earth.
16 Tula, the Toltec capital.
17 The last Toltec ruler, the one who gave the other prophecy quoted here
within the Cuauhtémoc's Legacy and which dates back to 500 years before
the *Legacy*. Ce Acatl Topiltzin Quetzalcoatl was born in AD 947 and disappeared in AD 999: traditionally he is regarded as the supreme achiever of the
Quetzalcoatl state.

come, like warmongering demons, to destroy our culture and break the law, killing and betraying their own gods.

The cross and the rattle of the snake[18] *shall mark the date with the sword, the bow and the arrow.*

The races shall mix like metal melted in clay pots. And so it shall happen.

Sign of the people sealed with the chimal [the shield] *of the warriors,*[19] *from Cuauhtémoc's consciousness the resurgence shall blossom again.*

The spirit of the eagle and of the rattlesnake shall carry our movement, both the movement of cosmic space and that between life and death.

Meanwhile we must all unite in Tloqueh in Nahuaqueh[20] *on Tlalticpac* [the Earth],[21]

transmitting the word of the Mexicas' origin and essence

to our sons and their progeny belonging to this generation and to the ones to come,

so that they come to know the beauty and harmony of Tenochtitlan

under the protection of our sacred essences, the energy that creates all that is,

the result of the education provided in our schools,

which our ancestors knew how to instil into our fathers and into our fathers' fathers,

who with great diligence educated the children in the streets and in the schools

to respect the mineral, vegetal, animal, human and solar-cosmic natures;

the commitment, with dignity and respect, to the universal consciousness;

18 Symbols used by the ancient Mexicas to measure time and movement.

19 The sign of this union will be the chimal, the shield of the warriors.

20 It is the energy, or essence, of the Inside and of the Intimate proximity, represented by a hand: every finger has its own function, each of them is equally important, but the best result is only achieved when they function both correctly and all together.

21 The intermediate world in which we live, in between the heavens and the underworlds, which corresponds to the centre of the flower, see Figure on page 5.

love for the family and for the common good: everything that must occur together, according to the law;
unity and honourable action on behalf of the nation, and the freedom of the new humankind.
With the advent of the Sixth Sun, Iztactonatiuh, the sun of balance ['the white Sun'] *shall shine and beget the sons of the Fifth Sun, the sun of Justice.*[22]
Like a new dawn, [new men] *shall come to rescue Anáhuac from the approaching future;* [they will do so] *for this is the will of destiny,* [they will do so] *with the dignity of our race and with the great* copal.[23]
At least let us leave behind chants, flowers and dances,[24] *so that the world of Anáhuac may continue to exist at this time.*[25]
The fame, glory and greatness of the beautiful Tenochtitlan, the continental capital of Anáhuac, shall not come to an end, in our loved and revered land of Anáhuac, where the winds so strongly blow".

12 August 1521 (according to the Julian calendar)
22 August 1521 (according to the Gregorian calendar)

Ometeotl!

22 This refers to the period between 1991 and 2021, e.g. the end of the Fifth and the rising of the Sixth Sun. See 'From the Dog to the Monkey', page 23.
23 An aromatic resin used as an offering.
24 Reference to the sacred chants and dances, and to the universe (the 'flowers').
25 In the transition from the Fifth to the Sixth Sun.

3 (YEI)

Ancient Mexico:
the Aztec and Mayan Calendars

Today we are witnessing a real global fever surrounding the
21 December 2012, a date based on the tzolkin, the Mayan calendar. This date has unleashed a whole host of mass reactions
characterized by all kinds of predictions and interpretations,
which have been triggering fear and paranoia. These range
from the possibility that the world may be coming to an end, to
a transition entailing all sorts of climate changes, to the likely
rotation of the magnetic axis, up to and including a whole series
of very painful events for humankind. In contrast to all this we
encounter the super-optimistic response of New Age supporters,
who talk in terms of a golden age for humanity.

Both approaches have primarily been circulated by authors
or researchers who have provided *their own* interpretation of
both the calendar and of the Mexican tradition. As for me, it is a
real honour to be the voice of my ancestors, and I have pledged
to transmit and share an authentic version of the Nahuatl culture
of Central Mexico, as it has been preserved by the guardians of
this tradition. To this day, they have been the custodians of the
calendar cycles, coupled with their cosmic mathematical measurements, and now this culture is ready to be shared with the
entire world in an effort to manifest the perfect union that exists
between the dance of the celestial vault, the cosmos, with its
constantly attuned rhythms and movements, and our daily life;
thus we shall come to appreciate how these cosmic mathematical movements affect both the behaviour and the consciousness

of the entire planet Earth, which participates in this dance.

My intention is to bring to light these authentic notions–which in Mexico continue to be taught by the guardians of the oral tradition–on the significance of specific dates and their relationship with both the 'essences' (the energies) and the planets, so that readers can be prepared for a personal transformation, just as I was prepared by my masters.

When compared with the oral tradition, some so-called academic texts, as well as some recent books that talk about our times and the return of Quetzalcoatl, or Kukulcan (two names used in the Nahuatl and Mayan languages respectively to indicate the same symbol of light and knowledge), seem to contain a number of distortions.

For instance, some academic texts state that Quetzalcoatl is either a god or a person whose return is expected by the natives; some more recent books, however, perhaps somewhat influenced by New Age ideas, talk of Quetzalcoatl as a new form of consciousness that is expected to self-manifest simply on the basis of an astrological conjunction connected with the rising of the new Sun.

The information that comes from the Mexica ancestors is simpler and more profound and significantly different: *Quetzalcoatl is viewed as a level of knowledge that can be reached on an individual basis following a personal training process, which can take place right now.*

Just as the cosmos in its eternal movement transforms itself while moving away from the shadow of the black *Tezcatlipoca*[26] to the light of Quetzalcoatl, from *Yohualli*, the darkness of the night, to *Tonalli*, the light of the day, similarly we too can transform the essence of our being, the 'cave of the black Tezcatlipoca' into the light of knowledge of the state of Quetzalcoatl. What does this really mean, beyond all metaphors?

This means that we can "train our perceptions" both in the waking state (*Tonal*), as well as in the sleeping state (*Nahual*), *so as to perceive what lies beyond the form.* Here the main thrust is that the prime essence of a being (*moyocoyani* in

---

26 The dark, initial state of everything that might come into existence; Chapter 9 is entirely devoted to this concept.

ancient Nahuatl) is simply an idea, which in its eternal movement can be replaced by a different idea... We can therefore recreate ourselves: while *Ollin*, the movement, brings the Sun, the Earth and the whole cosmos to a particularly special position, where they shall undergo a major change and transform themselves, *we too will have to proceed at the same pace and rhythm of the universe, as otherwise change will occur nonetheless, but its impact on us will be much more painful.*

How we can be aware of what is happening in the universe and how we can keep up with its pace, and therefore transform ourselves within the framework of this greater transformation, constitute the main topic of this book.

The reason why all this information is made manifest at this juncture, having been kept secret for such a long time, is that Cuauhtémoc's Legacy states that it is only in the Sixth Sun that it can come to light again in order to illuminate the consciousness–both in its waking and dreaming states–and thus awaken the dormant abilities which human beings are endowed with. And the Sixth Sun is rising right now.

I would like to point out that in this context the term 'prophecy' has a completely different meaning, in that it is not based on either oracles or predictions: instead it refers to a calendar, which is none other than a whole set of accurate and meticulous measurements of the behaviour of the cosmos, and of its interaction with the Earth. These measurements range from very short cycles which describe a single day to cycles of thousands of years describing the revolution of the Sun around the Pleiades. The longest cycle of the tzolkin, the Mayan calendar, will end on 21 December 2012, which is why many people have interpreted it as the end of the world, although many guardians hold a different view and maintain that the end of the cycle falls on 28 October 2011. We must remember, however, that all these calendars are both circular and cyclical, and therefore they repeat themselves.

Given that the Mayan calendar is soon coming to an end, it would be much more interesting to take a closer look at the Aztec-Mexica calendar which, although very similar to the tzolkin both in terms of dates and cycles, is considerably longer. Both Mayan and Aztec populations were forced to wander for a long time before they found a settling place: as far as the Aztecs are concerned, you may recall the tale of the seven tribes that left Aztlan, whereas the Mayans had to abandon their cities and sacred places because their local natural resources were becoming exhausted. In their pilgrimages–although taking place for different reasons and at different times–both nations were involved in observing and gathering all the available information on ancient Mexico, and their calendars are both based upon the earlier Mixtec-Zapotec calendar.[27] This was the product of those ancient civilizations that had settled in Oaxaca, in the Mexican Pacific region, and it accounts for the numerous similarities that exist between the two. The Mayan calendar, however, is formed of separate calendrical 'wheels' (the solar and the lunar cycle wheels, the long and the short cycle wheels, etc.), whereas the Aztec-Mexica calendar, which is the legacy of the great Nahuatl-speaking civilizations such as the Chichimecs, the Teotihuacans, the Toltecs and the Mexicas, gathers all cycles into a single wheel. This wheel summarizes in itself all the various aspects of the cosmic dance, spanning from one single moment up to incredibly long cycles as far as human consciousness and perceptions are concerned, which nonetheless represent a mere instant from the viewpoint of the All.

In this calendar, as shown on the next page, the first cycle is represented by a sun encircled by four figures: this is the essence of the knowledge of initiation that is part of Mexica spirituality.

One possible interpretation is that what appears to be the sun's tongue sticking out is actually the *tecpatl*, the obsidian dagger, namely 'justice' in the sense of mathematical precision or soundness, thanks to which we shall rapidly attain what we are going to create, or that which we have already created from our four states of consciousness, represented here by the four figures that encir-

---

27 The Mixtecs were one of the most ancient local populations and are behind the temple-cities that have now become well-known archaeological sites, such as Mitla and Monte Albán.

The Aztec calendar, also known as Toltec-Mexica

cle the sun: the waking state, the sleep state, the dream state and the state of death, which represent what our essence, or energy, creates both in the heavens and in the underworlds. It is therefore necessary to expand our own conscious perception to all those states that lie beyond the conscious or waking state, and this is precisely why we need to embark upon the required training, if we really want to "clean up our cave".

Detail of the calendar

The Four Columns of the Universe

The central figure in the calendar additionally represents time, which is created by the four forces, or columns, that support the universe: together they form the cosmic cross, i.e. a dynamic cross in perpetual motion. This movement is called *ollin,* and it constitutes the true nature of everything that appears to our senses, while the four dynamic forces create the unique essence of every single moment. These four forces, coupled with their dynamic outcome, which here is represented by the central sun, are called *nahui ollin*, or 'the four movements'.

The diagram within the central figure of the calendar, as you can see from the enlarged detail above, is always characterized by a dynamic nature, and it is composed of four ingredients, which together make up a fifth 'something': this is why in our tradition the number 4 is considered one of the sacred numbers.

These movements–which are present both within us as well as outside–can transform the course of our life in an instant, commencing with the darkness of our 'cave' (i.e. our potential, that moyocoyani that I have already mentioned): this rhythm of four elements that make up a fifth is like the eternal dance of transformation, like the music that rules the entire universe... we are referring to the creation of every single instant.

Our ancestors used to say that by knowing and understanding the rhythm of the universe and the four forces that support it men and women could become creators, as they would know how to exert their influence over each single moment. This was the purpose of Teotihuacan, the sacred site where to this day we can still admire the Sun and Moon pyramids, the place where people would learn how to create reality, which is why it continues to be known as 'the place where men become gods'.

This well-known diagram of a central sun surrounded by four figures carries therefore a number of different meanings, beside the creation of time:

- the 4 elements which make up everything, namely *Tletl* (Fire), *Ehecatl* (Wind), *Atl* (Water) and *Tlalli* (Earth), which–propelled by a subtle and unknown fifth element– create matter on Earth: we are looking at that time-space conjunction which we constantly experience in our daily life;
- the 4 lunar phases;
- the solar cycle (2 solstices and 2 equinoxes);
- the 4 main hours of the day (dawn, midday, sunset and midnight);
- and of course it also represents the previous 4 Suns. As you may recall, we are at the end of the Fifth, waiting for the Sixth to gain power.

From the Dog to the Monkey

Among all the cycles described in the Mexica calendar, the longest is formed by the sum total of millions of movements each lasting a single instant and all of a creative nature; this calculation is based upon the movements of the stars, the main one being–as you may recall–the revolution of our Sun around the Pleiades: as a matter of fact the Mexica ancestors regarded our Sun as the 8th Pleiade. This explains why the orientation of the majority of sacred sites is towards the Pleiades, which are the holders of the consciousness of the entire group. Our Sun, Tonatiuh, completes its orbit around them in 26,500 years, and this period of time is further subdivided into 'movements', or cycles, each lasting 6,625 years, which go under the name of 'Suns'. These Suns too are the holders of this group consciousness.

According to the Mayan calendar, 21 December 2012 coincides with the end of one of these cycles, the last one mentioned by the Mayans; it must be pointed out, however, that the Mexica calendar continues for at least another two Suns, that is to say another 13,250 years. In both calendars, one Sun does not begin at the very same time that the previous one comes to an end: there are in fact short transition periods during which they both coexist. Whilst the previous Sun is still ruling, the next one slowly begins to exert its influence, until the time comes when the two energies are equal; subsequently the old Sun gradually withdraws until the new Sun becomes the sole holder of the cycle. This happens in all natural cycles, such as in the passage from night to day, from day to night, from one season to the next, and in the phases of the Moon.

According to the guardians of the Mexica tradition, the transition we are currently facing started in 1991: the Sixth Sun entered the scene when the characteristics of the Fifth Sun, symbolized by *Itzcuintli,* the Dog, were still dominating; the power of the Sixth Sun, symbolized by *Ozomahtli,* the Monkey, started to gather strength in 2003. On 21 December 2012 the two Suns will have equal power, whereas from 2021 onwards a period of thousands of years will commence, during which humankind will be under the sole dominion of the Sixth Sun.

The shift of influence of the Dog to the Monkey represents a huge step forward for the evolution of global consciousness. In the cycle of the Dog, the laws of humankind were dictated by human beings, whereas in the cycle of the Monkey it will be nature that dictates its terms to us, and we can already observe how humankind will have to adapt its way of life to some great environmental changes.

The Cycle of the Pleiades and the 'New Fire'

Another shorter but equally important cycle is represented by the time it takes the Pleiades to return to their original position in relation to other stars (especially Orion) when observed from the Earth: this cycle lasts 52 years. Every year, on exactly the same day, celestial bodies return to their original position, except the Pleiades that instead accumulate an ongoing delay of 7 days per year, and this is why it takes 52 years before they can be seen again in the same cosmic location.

The Gregorian calendar is equally based on the movement of the Pleiades, which accounts for the year being divided into 52 weeks, each comprising 7 days: the mathematics of the cosmos is an integral part of our daily life, and people intuitively feel some hope for renewal around the date that each culture has earmarked for their New Year celebrations, when the cycle of 52 x 7 = 364 is completed. Different cultures have developed different methods to compensate for the missing day: in the Aztec calendar this adjustment is made by celebrating the new year once at midnight, the next year at dawn, the following year at midday, and the one after at dusk; in this way the missing day is accounted for over a four-year period. The Mayan calendar contains instead a 'day without time' (invariably the 25 July) in order to adjust to the Pleiadean cycle; whereas in the Gregorian calendar this adjustment is achieved by the leap year.

Thus every 52 weeks the possibility of personal renewal becomes a reality, and every 52 years the chance for a significant collective renewal is equally present, as represented in ancient Mexico by the 'New Fire' ceremony.

Fire is the element that, in addition to governing both the dream and sleep states, also governs the transformation to the waking state: *this means that we are given the opportunity to create a new personal dream each year, as well as a new collective human dream every 52 years.* The last New Fire at the time of the Mexicas was recorded by Chimalpain in the year *ome acatl xihuitl panquetzaliztli,* i.e. "two *carrizo* year,[28] *quet-*

---

28 The calendar years are subdivided into 4 types, which are repeated 13 consecutive times, and therefore after 52 years the cycle starts again. The *carrizo* years are one of these types and all New Fires are considered *car-*

zal feather fire", namely the year 1507; and the most recent in 1975, a decisive year, when the collective path for the next 52 years–which will end in 2027–was determined.

The Cycle of Tonatiuh and the 'Solar Waves'

Another important observation–of which the calendar acts as a reminder–is the rotation movement of Tonatiuh (our star) around its own axis, which lasts approximately 26 days; as a matter of fact, it is our star, the Sun, that governs human consciousness.

This rotation means that for 13 days in a row the Sun presents us with a kind of energy, or 'solar wave', which is followed by a different solar wave that expresses its polar opposite, in other words its dual aspect. Given that we represent the solar consciousness that has expanded on this Earth, we are consequently governed by these two opposite solar waves: the wave of the Sun of Quetzalcoatl (the sun of luminosity) and that of the Sun of Tezcatlipoca (the sun of darkness), which move according to the number 13, another sacred number connected with the Sun, as we shall see later.

According to the Aztec calendar, the day of birth of a human being is calculated by specifying their location along the solar wave, and it is expressed by a number that ranges from 1 to 13: this allows us to know how the Sun manifests within us, in both its auspicious and inauspicious aspects.

The initiation trainings for the dances and the breathing exercises are always connected with the numbers 4, 9, 13 and 52, which evoke the cosmic cycles present within us; the resulting rhythms effectively re-establish the cosmic order and restore the balance between our dualistic aspects. Some of these exercises will be explained in the following chapters.

The Cycle of Tonantzin, Mother Earth

In the Aztec-Toltec-Mexica calendar we also encounter those

---

rizo years; the name derives from a type of Mexican bamboo characterized by an inner cavity. Whoever is born under this sign, be it their year of birth, or a *carrizo* day or hour, is considered a promising ruler in that, as the saying goes, "the *carrizo* has no heart" (meaning that the heart is where passions are located, and therefore they would not govern impulsively).

cycles which illustrate the behaviour of *Tonantzin,* Mother Earth: if the influence of the Sun is expressed through cycles of 13, that of the Earth manifests through 18 cycles of 20 days, each of 20 hours, and every 20 days some subtler changes in the life of both nature and the Earth appear to take place. For instance, the seasons are divided into sub-cycles of 20 days, which present some specific features: the sub-cycle between 12 and 31 March is called *Atlacahualo,* or 'what the waters left behind', which refers to the time when the ice melts and rivers swell up, carrying with them a great abundance of everything: whoever is born in this period is defined by abundance, but equally by ambivalence, which is typical of water, which can either be destructive or constructive.

Obviously, there are similar descriptions for each of these twenty-day clusters.

18 cycles, each of 20 days, amount to a total of 360 days. The remaining 5 days are dedicated first to a recapitulation and then to the creation of the new year: just as through four movements governed by a fifth it is possible to exert some influence over each instant, similarly during these four days governed by a fifth (the so-called *nemontemis,* between 7 and 11 March, i.e. before the New Year) it is possible to exert influence over a whole year. The ancient 'men and women of knowledge' were well aware of this, and they were able to create the instant, the day, the cluster of either 13 or 20 days, the year, and could even predict longer cycles by observing the interaction between the Earth and the All.

The Glyphs of the Days

The 20 days are positioned along the calendar wheel as 20 glyphs, starting with *Cipactli,* the crocodile, the fundamental primordial energy, through to *Xochitl,* the flower, the most auspicious day for us to blossom. Consequently we are all born under the influence of a specific glyph, which on the one hand corresponds to some specific qualities of ours, but on the other hand relates to specific challenges that we will have to face and overcome in this life.

The glyphs are highlighted on the following page.

The glyphs of the days

The Venus-Moon Cycle

The calendar contains all this, and much more. For example, our consciousness in the sleeping state, the nahual, is governed both by Venus and the Moon, and the Aztec calendar contains several Venus-Moon cycles. In the waking state, given that it appears both at dawn and at dusk, Venus defines the Moon realm; in ancient times, well before the advent of electricity, people would fall asleep and enter their nahual in order to create their material world out of the subtle one. The Venus-Moon cycle tells us that it is necessary for us to sleep eight hours, if we do not intend to alter the vibration of the All: if we do not sleep well, or if we sleep less or more than 8 hours, we go against the rhythm and the movement of the universe, instead of going along with them. But where does this number 8 come from? One Venus cycle (i.e. the time it takes for Venus to go back to its original position, when observed from Earth) lasts 590 days, during which time 20 lunar cycles take place. Five of these Venus cycles give a total of 2,950 days, which divided by 365 results in the number 8. When we comply with this measurement, with this rhythm, we adjust ourselves to the rhythm of the universe, resulting in our wellbeing. The number 8 corresponds to our sleep, our shadow (the 'cave', that part of ourselves that is invisible), as well as to those cycles of individual renewal that occur every 8 years. All this is symbolized by the *quincunce*, the calendar figure just below.

590 x 5=2950
2950:365=8

The Venus-Moon cycle

Other Venus Cycles

In addition to the brief cycle represented by the quincunce, which only includes Venus and the Moon, there is another Venus cycle that accounts for the cosmos by using Venus as its reference point: this is the cycle of the 104 years required for Venus and the entire cosmos to return to their original positions when observed from the Earth. Once every two times this event coincides with the New Fire, which happens every 52 years. Although this cycle lasts 104 years, some masters prefer to talk in terms of 105 years, as the effect of this cosmic movement is only felt from the following year onwards.

If we wish to understand what change will take place in 2012, which will become even more clearly visible in 2021, it is necessary for us to develop a very clear understanding of how each instant of the physical world is created out of the subtle world, which goes by the name of the 'thirteen heavens', and how we create our tonal from our nahual.

Ometeotl!

Tonal and Nahual

If we want to understand what will happen in 2012 and our role in this cosmic mechanism, we must understand that the four movements also govern the most essential of all human aspects, namely our consciousness and perceptions.

Nahui ollin, the Four States of Perception and the Five Bodies

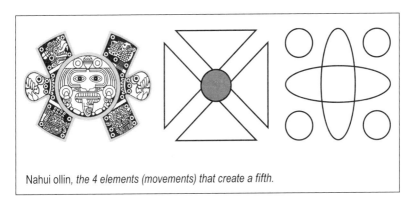

Nahui ollin, *the 4 elements (movements) that create a fifth.*

These figures represent the four forces that sustain the universe, whose interactions result in the perennial movement; as explained above, time comes from this interaction. Where do these forces come from, however? They come from the subtle worlds, where the physical and material universe comes to an end. They come from the mysterious world of the nahual, our consciousness of the sleep and spiritual state.

These figures encapsulate the highest form of knowledge of human nature ever achieved by pre-Columbian civilizations: how four energy bodies in movement (*tonal, teyolia, nahual* and *ihiyotl*, which will be discussed shortly) can give rise to a physical body (*tonacayo*) that is never the same, which is constantly self-renewing, and which changes and moves forward from moment to moment. In this physical dimension, traditionally these four subtle bodies are referred to as 'eggs' in the Aztec tradition and as *burbuja* ('bubble') in the Andean tradition, and more generally as 'aura' (see Figure below). These bodies are vehicles through which we can explore realities located well

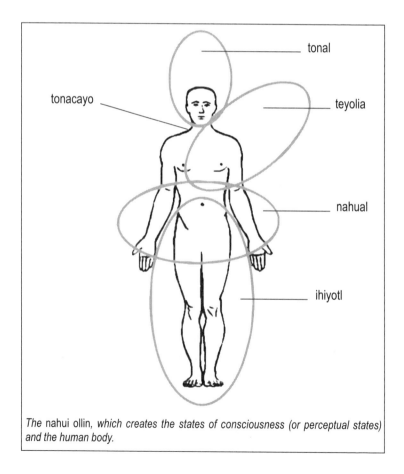

The nahui ollin, *which creates the states of consciousness (or perceptual states) and the human body.*

beyond the limits of the physical world. Their eternal movement is like a cosmic dance, which invents us and then reinvents us, which creates us and makes us continue onwards.

The interactions among these four energy bodies create both the physical body (*tonacayo*) as well as these four perceptual states:

- *waking state*: this state is characterized by sensations stemming from physical perceptions, when we are present to everything that is going on;
- *dream state while awake*: in its movement, this state is characterized by 'light', 'medium' and 'strong' variations. Light movements refer to when thoughts take us away from the present moment, medium movements correspond to the moment we enter into meditation or become involved in visualizations, and strong movements to when we enter into a deep state of trance and we begin to perceive the subtle worlds;
- *sleep state*: when our consciousness finds itself in an imageless state of dream, in which it penetrates only into the darkness of the moyocoyani, 'the prime essence of being' in the ancient Nahuatl language, and also called *amomati*, 'the empty mind';
- *sleep state with dreams*: namely the existence that we experience through our nahual in the *Temictli*, 'the place of dreams'; this has an influence on the creation of our tonal, the physical reality which we experience through the *tonacayo*, the 'physical body'.

These are the four common states of perception, which we are all familiar with; later we will discuss the non-ordinary state of *ensoñación*, or **dreaming while awake**.

Human beings are made up of these four ordinary states and of the following five bodies:

- *tonacayo*, or physical body;
- *ihiyotl*, the 'essence' or 'divine breath', the life force that comes from the subtle worlds and keeps matter alive. This energy comes into contact with us via the liver, an organ to which we must pay special attention in that,

according to this tradition, it is from here that *Miquiztli*, 'the force of death', having previously found its way in via the navel, extracts the ihiyotl; this is not a highly evolved, or sophisticated type of death, but incidentally it is the most common. Together with our nahual, the ihiyotl is the body, or vehicle, with which we move about both in the heavens and in the underworlds;

- *teyolia*, 'the energy around the heart', which protects the journey of our hummingbird, the journey of our soul: the memory and the number of all the lives that we have spent both in a physical as well as in a non-physical body (we can actually exist in the nahual without being present in the tonal). The Mexica tradition explains that if at death we exit the body via the liver, we are then forced to come back either as humans (namely in the case of an ordinary, less evolved type of death), or to proceed to the underworlds.

If we are unable to 'blossom' in life (meaning, if we are unable to discover and master the secrets of the flower that represents the universe), we will die exiting the body via the liver and we will have another opportunity to be born on the following day (or under the following glyph), and so on and so forth, until the cycle is completed (see Figure on page 28).

Unfortunately, however, the teyolia energy is not infinite: for instance, if people experience a great deal of suffering in their lives, they can use up much more energy of this type than in three or four peaceful lives. Once the whole energy of the teyolia body has been completely used up, if we have not yet been able to 'blossom', and have not learned at the very least how to die by exiting through the heart–which still does not constitute the highest place through which we could exit the physical body–we will not have any further opportunity to come back as humans, and will be forced to progress to the underworlds (i.e. the worlds that lie below), where everything is much more difficult and painful.

This is why all practitioners of this tradition, both in the past and nowadays, try their best to 'blossom' in this life, as nobody knows the amount of energy that they have left in their teyolia, and whether they may have one more opportunity to experience a human life.

We shall further discuss death and dying in Chapter 12, 'Death and the Nine Underworlds'.

The above does not mean that we only live up to a maximum of 20 human lives, as this cycle can be repeated: it all depends on the amount of energy that we are left with. And it goes without saying that the tradition also teaches us how to preserve our energy and gather more, which would naturally be channelled towards an attempt to 'blossom'.

How can the energy be preserved and how can we gather more?

We preserve the teyolia energy by limiting our emotions, our pleasures and our suffering; we then gather more energy by learning how to 'go hunting' for it, both in the waking and in the sleep states. This type of training can only be given directly and cannot be consigned to the pages of a book, because first students must learn how to transform those 'heavy energies' that they go hunting for into a type of energy from which to benefit.

Furthermore, if the energy that is accumulated through this kind of 'hunt' were not to be used to 'blossom' in this life (which once again would force us to exit the body through the liver), it would be totally used up in experiences of the kind that would noticeably drive us to that type of death.

In any case, it is preferable to use up the energy that has been gathered through this 'hunt' rather than the teyolia energy, as in this way at least less energy will be dissipated in the course of this life.

Being reborn under the same glyph, having accumulated knowledge and experience for at least 19 lives (if not longer), does not mean that we will be reborn under the influence of the same solar wave–which as you may recall is represented by a number ranging from 1 to

13–nor within the same cluster of 20 earth days; equally the time of day and the position at birth in relation to the Venus-Moon cycle and so forth will be different too. The initial conditions, therefore, will be totally different, and we will have a brand new opportunity: what will matter is whether we have accrued more experience as a result of the energy loss... which in any case is what happens regularly in each life of ours. We start off with plenty of energy and no experience, while at the end we have tons of experience but unfortunately there is no energy left!

The path that follows the wheel of the different glyphs will come to an end when we learn to die a 'glorious death', e.g., exiting the body at least through the heart to merge directly with the Sun, or when the teyolia energy runs out and we enter the Mictlan, the 'place of the dead', both of which will be discussed in Chapter 12, 'Death and the Nine Underworlds'.

- **Tonal**, the 'heat', is directly associated with the Sun. The whole physical universe, with all its forms and distances, is an illusory idea that has been engendered by our tonal, namely by that energy that is located around the head in the waking state, and which anyone who has trained in extrasensory perceptions can visualize easily: it covers the head and its colour is a matt amber-gold (although at the start of the training it is only visible as a golden light that surrounds the head). The tonal, however, swaps locations with the nahual when we are asleep, or in a state of trance: it then moves downwards from the head to the belly, while the nahual goes up starting from the belly and ends up reaching the head, which from the outside is perceived as an energy movement, and from the inside as the radical perceptual change that we experience when we move from the reality of the waking state to the dream state, or to an altered state of consciousness.

- **Nahual** comes from a Nahuatl root formed by *nehuatl*, 'I' and by *ni ye,* 'I am', and therefore it means 'who I really am'; it also comes from the word *nahualli*, meaning 'what can be extended'. It is a cold energy, which moves

in circular movements and resides in the navel area outside the physical body during the waking state, whereas
when we fall asleep it moves to occupy the location of
the tonal around the head, leading our perception to all
kinds of subtle worlds, i.e. to realities that transcend the
physical dimension. This is the sleep state consciousness,
or the consciousness of the state of trance, that state that,
for instance, in Spanish is called *ensoñación*, that **dreaming while awake** state which will be explained later. It is
equally that part of our energy that we can extend to the
point of reaching some other place and which, following
the correct type of training, can create an 'energy double'. At this stage I would like to take the opportunity to
clarify that the term 'nahual' does not mean either good
or bad sorcerer or mystic, namely the type who can either
heal or cause fear and panic among the people, or who
goes around saying to his disciples that the 'nahual is the
privilege of the few', as this could not be further from the
authentic tradition. The nahual is the governing energy
during the sleep state, and therefore we all possess a
nahual. 'Nahual' is however also the term used to refer
to whoever develops the power of this energy: the union
of the energy of tonal and nahual creates certain states of
consciousness through which it is possible to gain access
to the subtle worlds while awake, and to develop full mastery of lucid dreaming while asleep.

The 'nahuales' [plural of nahual, translator's note] can
thus unify the dream world, which is totally malleable,
with the world of apparent reality, where they manage to
manifest themselves in different forms just as in a dream;
they can then change this reality as easily as the actions
occurring in a dream. This gives them the amazing power
to influence and change matter.

The sages of ancient Mexico were 'nahuales': to become
a ruler it was necessary to know the cosmos, the *cipactonalli*, the 'language of what is known' [where 'known'
refers to the waking state, translator's note] and the *cipacnahualli*, the 'language of the unknown', and to know

who you were here (the tonal) as well as who you were
there (the nahual). Many of them would then become
healers.

The cipacnahualli is the symbolic language of dreams,
which can be learnt in exactly the same way as the language of the tonal: it is like another universe in which it is
necessary to learn how to move about. The cipacnahualli
is full of symbols, places, colours and beings, all different from the reality of the waking state; we all perceive
them in our dreams–although we have no recollection
of them–but only mystics and visionaries are capable of
bringing these experiences back with them when returning to the tonal and turning them into something useful.
Making sure that the nahual can become useful in the
tonal requires that the two become united, and this specifically necessitates an ancient form of training, which
is gradually re-surfacing in Mexico due to the influence
of the guardians of the tradition. This enables us to train
in controlling various states of consciousness, such as the
dreaming while awake, an altered state of perception
that is brought about by dances and breathing exercises,
without having to resort to sacred plants like the *peyote*;
from this state we can perceive the worlds of subtle energy, whilst remaining awake and fully conscious.

Another state in which tonal and nahual are united is the
sleep-dream-wake, or lucid dreaming, from which we
can exert complete control over dreams as a way of creating reality by means of the 'sowing of dreams', the subject
of Chapter 6, which talks about the thirteen heavens. The
passage from the *temictli*, 'uncontrolled dreaming', to the
temixoch, the 'blossoming of dreams', the 'controlled and
lucid dreaming of a master', who possesses the capacity to
sow dreams and make them 'blossom', is what everybody
should do in this life because, in the words of an ancient
Mexica proverb: "He who does not remember his dreams
is one of the living dead, as he does not have any control
over his own life." This gives us a sense of the importance
that the dream state held for the Mexican civilizations

before the Conquest: the scions of noble families and those destined to become warriors had this dream state control inculcated in them since childhood.

There is yet another state, called **dream towards the outside while awake,** from which it is possible to exert influence over others by altering their perceptions and, if really so inclined, altering their reality... And this is really what a nahual is able to do.

As time goes by and as the influence of the Sixth Sun keeps growing, we shall recover these abilities and we will be able to see much further afield, but this journey of conquest of ours will not be directed towards the outside: the time has come for us to return to the obsidian mirror[29] and set off to conquer ourselves.

The few oral and written sources available have preserved some of the sayings of the ancient *nahuales* or *nahualli*, the 'sages who united sleep and wake'; the main written source is the Florentine Codex, whereas others belong to the oral tradition called *mah toteotahtzin mitzmopieli*, 'the tale of our Venerable Land'. Here follows some examples:

- "The nahual is not weakened by emotions. It is not weakened by Coatzin's venerable snake, 'sexuality'". This saying seems to refer to the two different ways of becoming a nahual, one of which was through sexuality, while the other was through abstinence.
- "The word of the nahual is wise, he is the master of his liver, he serves the community, he is serious, frank and free of any excesses"; here the expression 'master of one's liver' might refer either to the ability of controlling one's anger, as the liver is viewed as the place where anger is created, or to the ability to travel to the heavens or to the underworlds by means of the *ihiyotl,* the life essence, the subtle body that is anchored in the liver.
- "The good nahual, reliable guardian, the one who observes, preserves, helps and does not damage anyone."

29 The obsidian mirror is one of the methods that allow someone who has been trained to gain access to different times and places, and thus widen his or her perceptions. See Chapter 8 for a full explanation.

- "The nahual is *tlamatini*, 'a sage', *mictlanmatini*, 'sage of the underworlds', *ilhuicatlmatini*, 'sage of the heavens'."

Given that it is also possible to develop one's nahual for misguided purposes, such as exerting control over others, another saying goes:

- "The evil nahualli is a spell holder, he casts a spell over people, he possesses spells to seduce people, he cheats people, he casts evil spells over people, he acts as an evil sorcerer against people, he makes fun of and upsets people."

The Subtle Bodies are not Exclusively Human
Thinking that this body that acts as the vehicle in the worlds of dreams, of death and of the subtle energy could be the exclusive domain of human beings would constitute a very arrogant mistake! All that exists comes from the highest heavens, therefore everything (sun and stars, day and night) is governed by the same order and is kept alive by a particular energy and spirit; it all possesses a measurable structure that can be observed within a specific cyclical calendar wheel, which describes both its presence inside the universe, in the waking world, and its counterpart in the worlds of sleep and death.

The extraordinary thing is that an expert in both the dream state and of those states in which perceptions are widened is even able to encounter the nahuales of the Sun and the Moon, of the Earth and of the animals in the subtle worlds; they can encounter the essences, or energies, of everything that lives in both the physical and subtle universes, and interact with them on an equal basis, in an exchange of power and knowledge, and thus influence the collective and individual reality of the waking state.

Amongst the disciples that I have had the honour to train, many have begun to unite tonal and nahual, thus transforming themselves into 'warriors of the sleep and waking states'; in their dreams they have encountered the essence of the Sun, Moon, Wind and Water, and upon requesting some form of change or healing, they have managed to obtain the requested result in the physical world.

For instance, I remember a woman from the United States who was taking part in one of my teaching tours around Mexico: in these tours, among other things, we work with dreams, and that night this woman had a dream in which the Sun appeared to her as a yellow-eyed Aztec calendar; this particular colour of the eyes is precisely one of those codes that stand to signify a dream encounter with the Sun.

The Sun invited her to contribute to the spread of this ancient knowledge and, notwithstanding the fact that this lady was in the process of planning her retirement, she decided to establish a centre devoted to the practice of this wisdom; later on she acknowledged that this project had given meaning to her life.

Ometeotl!

5 (MAHCUILLI)

The Mathematical Language of 'What is Known' (the Tonal)

The ancient oral tradition recounts that Cipactli, the oldest of all ancestral beings, who was shaped like a crocodile, was taken by surprise by Tezcatlipoca and Quetzalcoatl, two of the forces that support the universe. They opened his jaws wide and extracted a black and a white tree respectively, thus giving rise to dualistic existence, to that complementary nature which constitutes the philosophical basis and the fundamental principle of both Nahuatl and Mayan cultures. Everything invariably presents two complementary aspects, and this whole tradition is an attempt to maintain the balance between them.

Having given origin to creation, Cipactli also had to create the *tlahtolli*, namely the movement that spreads from the subtle worlds to the physical world by means of a mathematical order; this order is the basis of the cipactonalli,[30] the Nahuatl language[31] that is sacred because its onomatopoeic words still

30 The language of the waking state (translator's note).

31 Esteban, my own master Hugo's master, used to say that although the Nahuatl language was replaced by Castilian Spanish as the main language of Mexico, and was virtually eradicated within five hundred years, it would become again the most spoken language of Mexico after another five hundred years, on the grounds that this country's land has names and codes which still contain Nahuatl sounds, and this would therefore facilitate the recovery of this ancestral legacy. I was made aware of this prediction in 2006, and at the time I thought it was something extremely unlikely, and yet today Nahuatl has made a comeback in schools as an optional second language. Will Esteban's prophecy come true?

preserve the authentic vibration of what they represent, in addition to the initiation meaning of the *tlahtolli*, the order of creation. This very same order can be read in the pyramids and temples of the Nahuatl-speaking cultures, a perfect order, which creates new forms every moment. Cipactli equally created the cipacnahualli, i.e. forms and symbols that make up the language and communication of the subtle and 'unknown' world of the nahual, or sleep world, as you may recall.

The main task for humans lies in discovering both forms of this organised and precise language, i.e. both the sleep and the waking state forms, from whose union the 'blossoming' of humans shall arise.

If we fail to understand the meaning of these códices, in other words the meaning of this original language, any attempt to appreciate the great change that we are going to live through will be a useless exercise, in that this is where the key to identifying the difference between the First, the Second, the Third Sun, and so forth lies. This difference can only be understood when we learn the cipactonalli, the numeric or mathematical language of 'what is known', which is still utilized by Nahuatl-speaking people for counting purposes, and which for the mystics represents the explanation of how the entire illusion of the physical universe originates from the initial energy. This will give us a much clearer idea of the characteristics of the new Sun, which is governed by its own specific number (we are referring to the Sixth Sun), and which will allow us to foresee how humanity will generally behave under the forthcoming Sun.

The Numbers

●   *Ce* or *Cen* means 'one' or 'unity', from which comes the term *centeotl*, which is made up of *cen*, 'unity' and *teotl*, 'energy', which refers to the unique creative energy that carries in itself the original essence of everything, the generating principle which is also defined as 'what gives life, measure and movement to creation'.

●●   *Ome*, 'two'.
   This comes from the Nahuatl *omitl*, i.e. 'bone'. The original energy divides itself into two so as to create

everything, and as far as we humans are concerned, it is imprinted in our bones even before we come into this world. Traditionally it is thought of as a hollow bone, which is apparently divided into two by the hole, but which nonetheless remains one. Similarly in Cipactli's legend, the two trees become one, which represents how two opposite forces coexist in our life, just as in the case of the *yin* and *yang* symbol.

As far as human creations are concerned, the process entails introducing an intention into the generating principle (*centeotl*), which will imbue it with what it needs to manifest, namely life, measure and movement. This creative energy will initially penetrate into our bones, where the history of our land and of our ancestors is engraved.

From ome comes the word ometeotl, which you will find at the end of each chapter: this term means that the dualistic energy becomes united in accordance with a very precise order, before descending from the subtle worlds down to the physical one, to the Tlalticpac, the Earth, the place where we live. 'Ometeotl' is a word of power that moves the thirteen heavens, the nine underworlds and the four directions of our intermediate world, meaning the entire flower that symbolizes the universe (See Figure on page 5).

● ● ● *Yei*, 'three'.

This comes from the word *yeztli*, which means 'blood'.

For our ancestors, 'blood' meant the energy (*teotl*) of the universe in the subtle worlds, and it is to this symbolic use of 'blood' that the metaphor of *Xipe Totec,* the third force that supports the universe (which I will describe later), refers: every night it would skin itself, thereby shedding its skin and dyeing the Sun with the red of its blood, and the Sun in its descent would in turn make the land pregnant, guaranteeing in this way the rising of the new day. The Conquistadors failed to understand this metaphor and ended up being convinced that they were faced with actual human sacrifices.

When a human being who is familiar with the tlahtolli creates anything at this particular stage of the mathematical order that is followed by the creative process, the intention—which has already installed itself inside the bones during the previous phase—permeates the blood that is flooding the bone cavity; in this way it tunes into the ancestors, and thus heals the *mecatl*, 'the blood lineage', i.e. the family lineage. Later the desired effect will be produced in time and space, and it is thanks to our blood's energy that we can practically heal our entire family.

● ● ● ● *Nahui*, 'four'.

This comes from *nantli,* 'mother' and *hui,* 'order': 'the order of the mother', which obviously refers to Mother Earth.

Given that we live on this earth, anything that we might wish to create must necessarily exist on this planet, and must therefore be accepted by Mother Earth; at this stage our creative intention shifts from the energy of the blood to the bosom of *Tonantzin Coatlicue*, Mother Earth, so that she may be able to dream of it.

Our ancestors used to say that we human beings—who are made of the 'four-colour corn' (i.e. the four elements)—represent our Mother's most beloved dream.

━━━━━━━ *Mahcuilli*, 'five'.

This comes from *maitli*, 'the hand' and *cuilli*, 'worm' (but also 'fingertips').

In the process of creation, by the time we reach number five, the hand is complete; and the Earth, now that it has dreamt of this creative intention, adds strength to it by conferring abilities to the fingers of our left hand, which symbolize the worms that inhabit its bosom. This enables the hands to acquire the skills and abilities required to manifest our creative intent.

Here the Earth bestows upon us—who represent her dream—the power to create.

━━━●━━━ *Chicoacen*, 'six'.

This comes from the roots *chic*, 'power', *cóatl*, 'snake' (which equates to 'energy') and *cen*, 'unity'.

Number six represents the unification of the power of

energy, symbolized insofar as human beings are concerned by the term *Quetzalcoatl*. *Quetzal* is a sacred bird, but this word equally derives from the verb *quetza*, or 'elevate oneself'. In its initiation meaning it signifies that, when the energy rises up like a snake that passes through all our *totonalcayo*, or 'energy centres', the snake transforms itself into a *quetzal* and flies upwards, and this is the cause of our Awakening; this is why it is said that it is the Sixth Sun, i.e. the one we are about to enter, that will usher in 'the return of Quetzalcoatl', or better still of the *Quequetzalcoah*, in the plural, those who know how to transform their luminous energy into vitality and beauty, thus making the snake rise up to the point of transforming itself into a bird (the eagle, or quetzal), which is capable of flying up to the purest form of consciousness of the Sun and the subtle worlds. The training to achieve it all is one of the features of the forthcoming Sun.

●● ___ ***Chicome***, 'seven'.

This comes from the roots *chic*, 'power' (where the *c* stands for *ce* or *cen,* 'unity') and *ome*, 'duality'.

The meaning is 'the power of reunited duality' whose aim is to give rise to the tlahtolli, the required structural order that enables thinking to manifest in matter.

When training in keeping with the tradition, this number corresponds to the seventh energy level, out of which the creative act is made possible; we therefore transform ourselves into 'manifesters', those whom the ancestors used to call the 'people whose thinking is proven and established', the type of thinking that flies and knows how to manifest.

This is the number that leads us from the level of thoughts to the level of matter.

●●● ___ ***Chicuey,*** 'eight'.

This comes from the roots *chic*, 'power', *ce,* 'unity' and *onyei,* 'blood flow'.

This is the physical development of strength; it corresponds to the 'blood' (or energy) of the universe becoming active for the purpose of creating, and it comes from the four main cardinal points, namely North, South, East and West, and from the intermediate ones, i.e. North-East, North-West,South-East and South-West.

This energy touches our heart directly and can lead our teyolia to new experiences; furthermore, the number 8 connects us with our nahual, with our nahual-tonal duality, our light-darkness, by means of the Venus-Moon cycle, whose measurements can be traced back to the number 8 (See page 28 and onwards).

●●●● *Chicnahui*, 'nine'

This comes from *chic*, 'power', *ce*, ' unity', and *nahui*, 'Mother Earth's order'.

Number nine is also a sacred number, as it gives order to the eight directions of the universe in anticipation of creation. Inside Mother Earth we find the nine underworlds (our shadow, the unconscious), the nine destructive forces of our black Tezcatlipoca, to which is dedicated the whole of Chapter 9. Even if we know how to use the creative energy, it is still necessary to give it a specific sense and to invoke the universe, if we really wish that our creative intention reveals itself as manifest creation; if however our shadow energy counters it, this will make such manifestation impossible and, even before we can actually see the fruit of our creation, the creative intention itself will force us to heal both ourselves and our ancestors, and to restore the kind of mathematical cosmic order that it requires.

Before it can actually attain both knowledge and 'blossoming' (or enlightenment), which are possible under the auspices of the Sixth Sun, humankind will have to begin... from number 9, i.e. by 'cleansing' its own shadow, *which is precisely the goal of this book: to assist people throughout this transition so that they can manage to cleanse their shadow,* their 'cave', to borrow a word that is dear to our tradition.

There are many ancient techniques that aim to attain this goal, and the easiest to impart through the pages of a book makes use of breathing in accordance with the perfect mathematical order herein contained. You will find it on page 83.

Mahtlactli, 'ten'

This comes from *maitli,* 'hand' and *tlactli*, 'back': 'the back of the hand', as when we show the palm of our hand with its five fingers, and then we turn it to show its back and the 'other' five fingers, which are the complementary aspect of the previous ones. This is how we move from five to ten.

According to the tlahtolli, once we have cleansed our shadow and restored the order of the Earth, the shadow itself, just like the light, will contribute towards our creation, and the potential ability that was received at number 5 will actualize and manifest itself as real talent.

Mahtlactli once, 'eleven'

This comes from mahtlactli, 'back of the hand', *on*, 'and', and *ce* 'one'.

Once we have created something, our creative task is achieved and we need therefore to commence a new creative cycle to keep the movement going. If we invariably keep creating the same thing, this goes against the order or law of movement, which is why number 11 shows up in our lives to encourage us to move on to something else. How does it actually materialise? By means of problems! It may manifest either through financial difficulties, or through problematic relationships, or any other sort of personal difficulties. This is actually where humankind finds itself at present: with the advent of a new Sun, we are currently faced with a strong inner resistance to cleansing our shadow and changing the way we live. This is why we are now facing such dramatic collective challenges, such as global warming, new diseases, economic crises, and of course more earthquakes and tsunamis: our planet in turn is in the process of adapting to the new Sun, and this process entails cleansing her shadow... a good deal of which is represented by the mess that we have created due to our ignorance.

Those who have been initiated to this ancient knowledge

are well aware of how necessary it is to keep flowing constantly, to keep renewing ourselves and creating new universes and experiences so as to truly 'blossom'.

Mahtlactli omome, 'twelve'

Omome means 'and two' and includes *ome* which, as we already know, means 'two' and 'complementarity'.

This is the energy level that humankind will only reach in 40,000 years from now, with the Twelfth Sun; nonetheless those who manage to transform the shadow into light and knowledge by following the right discipline will be able to attain this level even now and acquire the full understanding (and perfect mastery) of complementary duality: tonal/nahual, life/death, light/shadow. They will be able to use both energies to attain anything they desire, including the immortality of their own energy; they will overcome their ordinary destiny, which in our tradition refers to being absorbed either into the light (when the type of death enables us to unite with the Sun) or into the shadow (when after death we find ourselves in the underworlds, deprived of our individuality). Only those who reach the level of 12 are therefore able to choose the survival of their individual energy, an option denied to the overwhelming majority. An extremely small number of people will be able to melt with the light, whilst the majority will be absorbed into the shadow, having passed through the suffering of the underworlds. One is a joyful end, while the other is painful and sorrowful. When the Sun is in turn sucked into a black hole, all the light shall be absorbed by the shadow, out of which however the light shall be born again, in this eternal complementary movement.

Mahtlactli onyei, 'thirteen'

Onyei means 'and three'.

This is the number of the heavens (see Chapter 6) and of those who know them and who through them are actually able to create, both in the dream state and within matter.

It is the number of the solar wave, of the cosmic blossoming and of the spectacular death that entails either merging with the light or maintaining one's own individuality: according to our tradition, this is a personal decision. This is the number of Quetzalcoatl, the 'grand finale' that is reached only after having lived a life full of knowledge and beauty, of 'flowers and chants', as our ancestors used to say.

It is only now that the training and the knowledge underlying such a momentous achievement are coming out into the open: it has neither happened before, nor will it occur afterwards, because the prophecy states that they are needed NOW.

We have embarked upon a transition towards a new cycle, and therefore we need to understand what is going on and how to make the best use of the present time.

This is the legacy that Mexico, once known as Anáhuac, can offer humanity as a whole.

Ometeotl!

6 (CHICOACEN)

The Thirteen Heavens and the Creation of Each Moment

The thirteen heavens are to be understood as thirteen distinct dimensions, or 'layers' of existence, which describe the process of creation and the movement of the All. They are also a tangible example of the profound knowledge of the ancient Mexicans of how manifestations would unfold; starting from the centre of Teotihuacán, where it was said that "men and women would transform into gods", this knowledge would pass through the Toltecs and subsequently from them to the Mexicas. This description shows us how the physical world is generated from the subtle worlds in a perfect balance and how it is possible to directly influence the creative process, instead of limiting ourselves to the role of simple spectators, or of confining ourselves to being the outcome of such processes. Those who are trained would therefore learn how to modify their surrounding reality, i.e. both the animal and plant worlds, by means of their consciousness.

Such a cosmogonical concept includes the nine *chicnahuilhuicatl,* the 'subtle heavens', four material or physical heavens (the last one being the Tlalticpac, the dimension in which we live: see Figure on page 5), and the *chicnauhmictlan,* or 'underworlds'. With their energy, the nine subtle heavens and the nine underworlds feed the four physical heavens, including the Tlalticpac, thus forming two energy flows: a warm flow made of light and a cold one made of shadow. Their perfect balance brings about the balance that is present within the complementary duality.

The current world situation, which is extremely dualistic, is caused by two factors: the increase in the light that comes from the skies above, due to the increased solar activity that characterizes this transition to the new Sun, and the release of a higher amount of shadow energy by the underworlds to balance this increased quantity of light.

This view of the world is often symbolized by a tree:

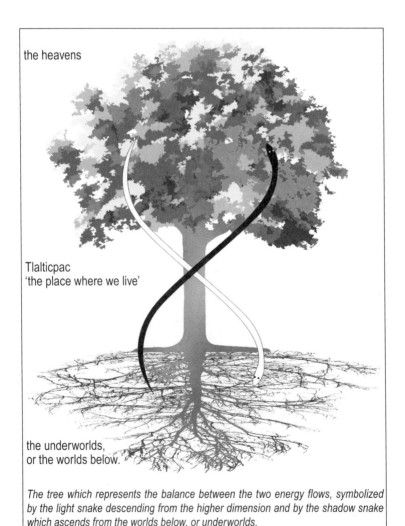

the heavens

Tlalticpac
'the place where we live'

the underworlds,
or the worlds below.

The tree which represents the balance between the two energy flows, symbolized by the light snake descending from the higher dimension and by the shadow snake which ascends from the worlds below, or underworlds.

The description of the thirteen heavens represents one of the most sophisticated explanations of how the energy descends from the subtle worlds down into the matter based upon a certain order, measure and movement, which make this space-time synchronization possible.

This order is as follows:

Mahtlactli onyei ilhuicatl, 'the Thirteenth Heaven'

The name of this heaven is *Cehonomeyohcan,* 'the place where our lineage is united': this is the location of the primary energy, *centeotl,* the essence of all that exists, which is not created, it is self-invented and cannot be destroyed by anything. Our individual component of this essence is moyocoyani (see pages 18 and 33). Each heaven manifests in some form or other in the physical universe, and the thirteenth appears briefly in our reality both as the darkest hour of the night, i.e. just before dawn, as well as corn, regarded as the essence of the creative energy within the plant world. The oral tradition states that corn is the outcome of a type of human creation based upon the knowledge of these thirteen heavens, which is why there are four varieties of differently coloured corn, representing the four cardinal points: black, golden, white and red corn. This food contains the power and essence of the four directions, the type of energy that we can absorb by eating these four varieties of corn.

Mahtlactli omome ilhuicatl, 'the Twelfth Heaven'

This heaven's name is *Ohonomeyocan,* 'the place of complementary duality', although nearly all sources mistakenly refer to it as *Omeyocan,* a name that has two roots: *ome,* 'two', and *yei,* 'three': given however that 2 x 3 = 6, this 'word of power'[32] is actually the name of the Sixth Heaven, and can only invoke its corresponding energy.

The name *Ohonomeyocan* adds instead one more 2 (2 x 2 x 3 = 12), taking us to the most subtle most realms, to the prime location of original duality, where the primordial energy is divided into two: *Omecíhuatl,* and *Ometecuhtli* (literally: 'Mrs and Mr. Two'), which

---

32 'Words of power' are sounds that produce an immediate energetic effect; they are also used to invoke a specific type of energy.

equate to the yin and yang of other traditions, often shown in the códices as two people who, through their speech (the Word) and by smoking tobacco (the divine breath), give shape to creation.

Omecíhuatl and Ometecuhtli, literally 'Mrs. Two' and 'Mr. Two'.

Before and after reciting the supplication prayer during ceremonies, as well as inside the 'temazcal baths' (the Mexica tradition's 'sweat lodge' shaped like an igloo, see page 88) for instance, the words *ometeotl* or *omeyocan* would be pronounced, whose meaning is "may what is dual unite in order to create" and again "may what is created in the subtle world manifest in the physical realm", which is a reference to the Sixth Heaven. However, the great masters are well aware that by adding the syllable *oh* the prayer will be much deeper and more effective, and will reach the Twelfth Heaven: this is why they recite *ohometeotl*, or *onometeotl* or even *ohomeyocan*.

One part of the energy of the Twelfth Heaven is the *ontlaixco*, or 'the place of lofty thinking', creative original thinking, divided into a feminine and a masculine aspect, namely into 'father-thought' and 'mother-thought', which are depicted by two parallel lines running respectively from East to West and from West to East.

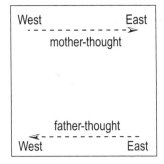

The energies located between the Sixth and the Twelfth Heaven are commonly named *onahcopa*, i.e. 'what rises up' and are depicted by two vertical lines that rise upwards to unite the father-thought with the mother-thought, thus forming a square, which symbolizes Earth, time and matter.

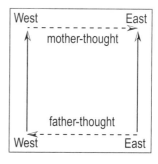

At a mythical level, *Omecíhuatl* and *Ometecuhtli* are depicted as humans, and give birth to four sons or energies, the four Tezcatlipocas, the four columns that support the universe, which correspond to the four corners of the square that sustains creation.

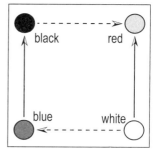

Tezcatlipoca comes from *tezcatl*, 'mirror', and *poca* 'smoke', thus meaning 'smoking mirror', i.e. the creator of matter and what cannot be seen clearly.

Each of these energies or essences called 'Tezcatlipoca' are first of all expressed on the spiritual level, then on the cosmic-astronomical, and lastly on the human level, in the Fifth Heaven, giving rise to all subtle and physical creations. The Toltecs, the Mexicas and the Mayans were experts at discovering the synchronicity existing between the subtle spiritual energy, astronomical phenomena and human consciousness, and this is the basis of their measurements and predictions of the influence of cosmic cycles over our lives, as illustrated by the calendar.

The Four Tezcatlipocas
- The first born 'child' (or energy) is *Yayauhqui Tezcatlipoca*, 'the black Tezcatlipoca', the most famous and most worshipped essence, or energy, of ancient Mexico; on a spiritual level, it represents the primary individual

energy that manifests out of the undifferentiated *centeotl*; it transforms into an idea, which subsequently develops into individual beings, be it humans or
animals, planets, stars, etc. Astronomically, the black
Tezcatlipoca corresponds to the centre of the galaxy,
and its female equivalent is the Moon and the night;
on a human level, its correspondence is the 'cave' (the
unconscious), which can either give us everything or
take it all away from us, which is the source of either
good luck or misfortune, and which can either express
the highest values or the greatest destruction; we are
permanently in the middle of this force and, by first
making the shadow visible by means of our instincts
and reactions, or by cleansing it, we are able to decide,
moment by moment, which of the two polar opposites
we want to experience.

- The second born child is *Tlatlauhqui Tezcatlipoca*, 'the
red Tezcatlipoca', known as *Xipe Totec*, 'the essence of
renewal', or of fertility. He is the outcome of the particular inclination of the first Tezcatlipoca towards a specific
pole: either pleasure or pain, peace or suffering and so
forth.

Astronomically it corresponds to the Milky Way, and on
a human level to the renewal that relates to the inclination of our unconscious (the first Tezcatlipoca): it renews
us by producing change, which manifests as patterns that
may resemble what we have previously experienced, or
may be completely new, but which in any case are in constant movement, even when they do not appear to be.

When we decide to cleanse our black Tezcatlipoca, this
renewal manifests through completely new patterns: whoever has completed such process will either heal, or will
totally drop all destructive behaviour that may have been
occurring for years.

- The third born is *Texouhqui Tezcatlipoca*, 'the blue
Tezcatlipoca', also known as *Huitzilopochtli*: on the spir-
itual level this is the essence of discipline and repetition.
On both astronomical and human levels repetition makes

universe and humankind predictable: it is the essence that creates those temporary cycles that allow the calculation of solar, lunar and earth periods.

- When a repetitive cycle becomes interrupted as a result of acting from the dimension of the black Tezcatlipoca, this leads to different renewals (red Tezcatlipoca) being produced, which repeat in an orderly fashion for a specific time (blue Tezcatlipoca), until a totally different creation takes place, or one that might appear identical to the previous one on the human level (depending on the inclination of the black Tezcatlipoca). Astronomically the blue Tezcatlipoca is represented by the morning Sun and by the planet Mars.

- The fourth and last is *Quetzalcoatl*, 'the white Tezcatlipoca'; spiritually this means that the experience that has been lived becomes knowledge. Astronomically it is symbolized by the midday Sun and the planet Venus, while on the human level it manifests as the experiences that we accumulate according to the model which I have previously illustrated:

  1. our unconscious, the black Tezcatlipoca, makes us incline towards a specific polarity;

  2. the red brings about our renewal by means of patterns that are either similar or completely different from the previous ones;

  3. the blue, the Tezcatlipoca of discipline, ensures that we experience these patterns in repetitive cycles within the time dimension;

  4. the white Tezcatlipoca, the level of a *Quetzalcoatl,* is the result of this entire creative process, which in our life provides us with knowledge and wisdom as products of experience.

The four Tezcatlipocas are present in many other heavens, in as much as their powers manifest in the creative process.

Mahtlactli on ce ilhuicatl, 'the Eleventh Heaven'

The name of this heaven is *Teteocan,* 'where the gods abide', and it is the location of the spiritual energy of the four Tezcatlipocas, which from here project themselves to other locations.

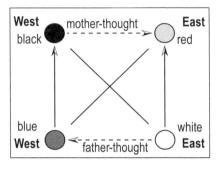

Their four colours transform into father-thought and mother-thought colours, which become united to create all types of perfect geometrical forms, before projecting into the physical world. Inside the square, the interaction of these four forces creates *onmaxal*, or *ohmaxal*, the 'cosmic cross', or the 'dynamic cross', whose movement gives the appearance of a circle, as with

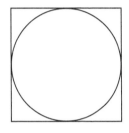

a fan. The geometrical symbol of creation is therefore a circle contained within a square.

Mahtlactli ilhuicatl, 'the Tenth Heaven'

The name of this heaven is *Tlatlauhqui ilhuicatl,* 'the deep red sky of wisdom', where the tlahtolli is created. This is the mathematical order that governs all that exists, ranging from the infinite sky to every single moment, from the entire universe down to each individual being: this is the order that is described in the calendar. Its brief presence in our physical reality appears in the red sky at sunset, which for us acts as a reminder.

Chicnahui ilhuicatl, 'the Ninth Heaven'

The name of this heaven is *Texouhqui ilhuicatl,* 'the deep blue sky of the cycles'. From a numerological standpoint the energy that resides within the black Tezcatlipoca is in direct relationship with the nine underworlds, and both the black Tezcatlipoca and the underworlds give rise to repetitive patterns that manifest both at the astronomical and the human level. In this heaven we see the creation of temporary cyclical movements that can only be altered by acting from the dimension of the pure essence of beings, that is to say, from the level of the black Tezcatlipoca.

In our world the manifestation of the 'Ninth Heaven' is the perfectly blue sky that appears very frequently in Mexico and is a constant reminder of a particular behaviour being repeated. Sometimes I wonder if the Mexicas had settled in Britain, the corresponding symbol might have been a grey sky, which is most common there, and the only one that keeps repeating...

Chicuey ilhuicatl, 'the Eighth Heaven'

The name of this heaven is *Coztic ilhuicatl*, 'the golden sky of the Spirit of the Sun', the Sun's consciousness which comes before its manifestation on the physical level; there are various aspects of the Sun's spirit that in our culture are depicted through the four Tezcatlipocas, and one of them is Quetzalcoatl, the one who gives humans their consciousness and knowledge. Human consciousness comes from the Sun, in that man is viewed as dust that belongs to this star, in human form. In this case the essence of the Sun transforms into *Teyocoyani*, 'the one who invents people', from which comes the legend of the Sun as the creator of humankind.

Given that we are solar consciousness, we fall under the influence of its cycles, and the representation of this sky in our physical reality is the summer solstice, when the Sun metaphorically transforms into an eagle (a crucial day to experience one's transformation into a 'man of knowledge'), as well as the winter solstice, when the Sun is metaphorically born as a hummingbird to initiate the renewal process.

In this sky there is a place called *Iztlacoliuhqui*, 'where the obsidian daggers clash', a metaphor used to illustrate the kind of storms that affect Tlalticpac, the place where we live, which reminds us that ancient populations were already aware of how water evaporation and the winds, the cause of these storms, come from solar energy and its activities.

Chicome ilhuicatl, 'the Seventh Heaven'

The name of this heaven is *Iztac Ilhuicatl*, 'the white sky of the Spirit of the Moon': here too, the consciousness or spirit of the Moon is on a level that comes before its physical manifestation; and since *Metztli*, the Moon, is the feminine representation of the black Tezcatlipoca, her influence is exerted over our nahual and our dream world. This sky is associated with the number 7, which in cosmic mathematics corresponds to the creation; we therefore know that, based on this cosmic order, it is the dream that creates the physical reality, and not the other way round. For a neuroscientist, it is the brain that creates the images contained in our dreams, whereas for a mystic of this tradition, it is the dream that creates the physical world, brain included! Hence the necessity to gain control over what we do in the nahual, by developing the ensoñación or **dreaming while awake**, one of those altered states of consciousness I have already mentioned, and the **sleep-dream-wake**, or **lucid dreaming**, which makes possible the meeting with the spirits of all that exists, be it in the physical or subtle dimension: we can encounter the Sun and thus change humankind, or meet the Moon and trigger off specific dreams. The Seventh Heaven is the location of temictli, the land of dreams, from which we can have access to temixoch, i.e. 'lucid dreaming' or 'blossomed dreams'.

In our reality this Seventh Heaven manifests as the white of the Moon and the darkness of the night, which stand for the complementary duality of tonal/nahual, which we need to learn to balance.

One traditional Mexica training technique teaches how to 'sow dreams' by following some precise codes which subsequently produce results on the physical reality level; it is very exciting to listen to the tales of whoever dreams of what they had previously sown, followed by the material appearance of the dream, as in the case of the following testimony provided directly by the protagonist of this experience, in a radio interview in Mexico.

A girl from Mexico City who had been suffering from a self-immune condition that caused severe sores on her feet to the point that she could not wear anything but a pair of sandals sowed a healing dream in herself, in which she was to meet a golden owl. She had attended a specific training of mine and when a few weeks after the 'sowing' she actually managed to dream of this owl, she was able to maintain her lucidity throughout the dream and to recognise that it was the actual symbol of healing she had previously sown. That very morning she woke up without the usual pain: her illness had disappeared and from that day on she was able to wear all types of shoes again. This stands to confirm the Toltec wisdom that says: "life is a dream and dreams are the creator of life..."

Chicoacen ilhuicatl, 'the Sixth Heaven'

The name of this heaven is *Omeyocan*, 'the place of second duality', and it is here that the square started in the Twelfth Heaven comes to completion: the parallel lines of father-thought and mother-thought unite with the ascending energies that emanate from the Twelfth Heaven. Energy and matter converge inside this square, which represents the Earth. As we have already seen, this is the heaven that ometeotl, the most used word of power in the Nahuatl language, makes reference to: this word therefore activates the energy in an upward and downward direction, by means of the movement of the cosmic cross located within the square.

In our physical reality, this sky is expressed by the two transition periods of dawn and sunset.

Mahcuilli ilhuicatl, 'the Fifth Heaven'

The name of this heaven is *Ollin Ilhuicatl,* 'sky in motion'. This is where we find the complete square diagram that contains the cosmic cross in motion, called *onmaxal* or *ohmaxal*, 'the convergence of all subtle forces', which keep creating on a continuous basis, thus giving birth to each instant. It is the central figure of the calendar, the basis of the entire view of the world expressed through the various *nahui ollin* symbols which–as we now realize–are the four Tezcatlipocas, the creators of all that exists.

The cross is the cause of the movement of two wheels: one that moves in a clockwise direction and represents the movement of the nahual, the other that moves in an anticlockwise direction, representing the tonal movement; the latter is also the direction in which the calendar is to be read. See next page.

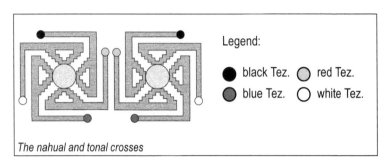

Legend:

● black Tez.   ◐ red Tez.

◓ blue Tez.   ○ white Tez.

The nahual and tonal crosses

If the essence of what we are (our black Tezcatlipoca) leans towards what the ancient tradition defines as *yaotl*, 'the enemy', then Xipe Totec (our red Tezcatlipoca), will create a destructive order in our nahual, and therefore our tonal shall contain some destructive patterns that we repeat in an orderly fashion (Huitzilopochtli, the blue Tezcatlipoca) until we experience destruction and suffering, which in any case will eventually turn out to be knowledge (Quetzalcoatl, our white Tezcatlipoca).

If, however, our black Tezcatlipoca leans towards the lofty and exquisite shadow of what the tradition calls *Nezahualpilli*, 'he who has defeated all his weaknesses' (which will be further discussed in the Chapter 9 dedicated to the black Tezcatlipoca), in that case Xipe Totec, the red Tezcatlipoca, will create a constructive order in our nahual, and our tonal will contain constructive patterns that will be repeated cyclically over time in an orderly fashion (thanks to Huitzilopochtli, the blue Tezcatlipoca), until we attain the human 'blossoming', namely the luminous knowledge of Quetzalcoatl.

In our physical dimension, the Fifth Heaven is associated with the appearance of comets, called *citlalli popocas* ('smoking stars') in Nahuatl, of stellar rain and moving stars, i.e. where cosmic movement is noticeably fast.

Nahui ilhuicatl, 'the Fourth Heaven'

The name of this heaven is *Cincalco ilhuicatl,* 'the sky of the stars'. This is where, with the exception of the Pleiades, all the stars are located, grouped into two sets: the four hundred Northern and four hundred Southern ones, like two armies facing each other and reflecting the complementary duality of ometeotl and of the whole universe, the reason behind the alternating cycles of light and darkness. We must bear in mind that in this tradition 'darkness' does not mean 'evil', but rather 'gathering' (i.e. turning the gaze inwardly) and that light means to see what lies outside, just like in the daytime and at night.

Yei ilhuicatl, 'the Third Heaven'

The name of this heaven is *Tianquiztli ilhuicatl* or *Tlahuizcalpantecuhtli ilhuicatl*, 'the sky of the Pleiades and the great star Venus'.

The movement of the universe in relation to ourselves is guided by the Pleiades and by the revolution of our Sun around them; as we know, the result is this huge cycle of 26,500 years, which is divided into four periods, or 'Suns', each lasting 6,625 years, and further shorter cycles each lasting 52 years, going by the name of 'New Fire' periods. All these cycles have a profound effect on our global consciousness and will produce momentous changes for both humankind and the planet as a whole. There are other changes that take place on the basis of the 105-year cycle[33] of the so-called 'Venus' return', when we observe them from down here on Earth: we perceive them as the turn of the century that causes humankind to develop and progress; furthermore, and in conjunction with the Moon, Venus also produces 8-year cycles, which bring about personal changes.

Ome ilhuicatl, 'the Second Heaven'

The name of this heaven is *Tonatiuh ilhuicatl,* 'the sky of the Sun'. This is where the Sun moves about, that Sun which gives us life, which rises every day and that at every sunset makes the West, the female cardinal point, pregnant, so as to give birth to the next dawn. It is through the Sun that we can achieve our most glorious destiny, the level of consciousness of a *Quetzalcoatl*, and then at death either melt with the Sun itself or choose to keep our individuality, like a nahual or an avatar.

---

33 I would like to remind readers that, although the Venus cycle lasts 104 years, some masters prefer to talk in terms of 105 years, as the effects of 'Venus' return' are only felt from the subsequent year onwards.

Its power is symbolized by the *tecpatl,* 'the flint knife', and the fact that the Sun is in the Second Heaven is an indication of its duality: it can express itself either as the Sun of Quetzalcoatl, which gives life, warmth, knowledge, justice and enlightenment, or as the Sun of Tezcatlipoca, which causes drought, destructive winds, hurricanes, earthquakes and personal catastrophes.

Ce ilhuicatl, 'the First Heaven'

The name of this heaven is *Metztli ilhuicatl,* 'the sky of the Moon', where Moon and clouds move about.

Few people, Mexicans included, are aware that the word 'Mexico', of Nahuatl origin, means 'the location of the Moon's navel' and that the Mexica culture was most highly specialized in the study of lunar cycles and of their influence on humans, and therefore also in the study of the influence of dreams over the same physical reality.

This is why, although also developed in the Mayan culture as well, nahualism is almost exclusively confined to the Toltec, Teotihuacan and Mexica cultures, the great specialists of in both the dream and dreaming while awake (*ensueño*) states.

The development of these studies was such that historically it gave rise to two main categories of warriors: **the eagle-warriors** and **the jaguar-warriors**. The first group developed the powers of the tonal, of the waking state and of the physical body. For instance: while in their waking state they would enter into altered states of consciousness by means of suitable training (breathing exercises, dances, etc.), from which they could even manage to bring back extremely heavy objects, as if in a dream, they would blend the two worlds of tonal and nahual into one, and in this way they would carry out the most impressive physical activities. The oral tradition maintains that they were even capable of flying, hence the origin of their name.

The jaguar-warriors, on the other hand, would develop the forces of the night, the universe of the nahual and of the under-worlds, and in this way they could penetrate into everyone's dreams and fight in their sleep. They could either kill or injure the nahual, the energy body of their opponent, in exactly the same way as in battle. When they succeeded in doing this, they

Jaguar man, Cacaxtla, Mexico. Detail of the fresco.
See colour insert.

would injure the enemy, who would then not last long. The eagle-warriors were therefore forced to learn how to fight and defend themselves while dreaming, whilst the jaguar-warriors had to learn how to fight in the physical reality. In Cacaxtla, an archaeological site located in the State of Tlaxscala, not far from Mexico City, there is a fresco illustrating the battle that took place between eagles and jaguars, which was won by the eagles.

One of the training centres or schools for both eagle and jaguar-warriors was located in Malinalco, in Mexico State. Throughout the Aztec empire, whoever was destined to become either a warrior or a ruler would be separated from their family as a child, and would receive training of both a military and spiritual nature, somewhat resembling the training which in the East was reserved for samurai warriors. This was not part of the regular Mexica army, rather of what nowadays we would label 'an elite force'. These warriors could have easily defeated the conquistadors, but they themselves were aware of the prophecy; and, as we know, when Motecuhzoma did not authorize them to go into battle, they committed suicide to avoid becoming slaves in their own country.

The First Heaven, being the closest to us, also constitutes the biggest challenge to our species, the most definite expression of duality; and the Mexicas discovered that it was linked to the Moon, which makes the waters move.

This is the home of *Tlaloc,* the essence or energy of Water, which can either manifest itself as fine drizzle or as a dreadful deluge; and human emotions, our water, are exactly the same, in that they can cause either pleasure or pain, love or hatred and any other dualistic emotion. With its phases, the Moon makes our dreams dynamic and, once we have developed the ability to control the nahual, it can either induce beautiful and healing dreams, or destructive ones; these will create the reality of our tonal, based upon the content of our dreams.

We could, for example, be talking about the dream of an artist, which is subsequently shaped into a work of art, or of the destructive dream of a genocidal maniac.

This is the same heaven where the duality of *Ehecatl,* 'the Wind', resides; it is the wind that moves clouds and water, and it can similarly bring about great blessings, as in the case of the yellow wind from the East, or the tragedy of sickness and death, such as it happens with the black wind from the North. Having lost touch with nature, we no longer heed the messages that come with the wind, which actually acts as an intermediary between dreams, where we create most of our life, and reality. If we have created something positive, a gentle wind from the East will be the harbinger of its manifestation, whereas in the case of something negative, a strong wind from the North will warn us of the impending tragedy: this is why in Mexico they still give the name *norte,* i.e. North, to all damaging storms. If, however, we know how to heed the message that blows with the northerly wind, we can still do something to avoid any potential disaster.

Our wise ancestors noticed that dreams, emotions and winds keep humans locked inside an invisible jail where they are forced to live the most intensive form of duality: good health and illnesses, life and death, happiness and sadness, pleasure and pain, and so forth; this prevents them from seeing beyond, from seeing the sun of their own Quetzalcoatl. And they named this condition of ours 'the prison of the Moon'.

Those sages then decided to smash this prison down and to command the wind, taking control of both their destiny and of their dreams so as to 'dream again' (i.e. change their dreams to change their reality) and in so doing meet the essences, or pure energies, and create together, in conjunction with them; they decided to take charge of their emotions and sexual energy, instead of being at their beck and call, and to save up this type of energy so as to rise further up towards the Sun, until they could meet their own Quetzalcoatl.

Knowing how to destroy the prison of the First Heaven is the gift that my ancestors have bequeathed us as their legacy for this time, when the world must awaken. With the advent of the Sixth Sun, these teachings have actually become available and are being practised again, so that new *Quequetzalcoah* (in the plural), of all gender, colour and ethnic origin, can manifest and smash down this prison, and meet their sun both in their dream and waking states alike.

It is for this reason that the first technique that I share in my seminars all over the world is 'The Sacred Breathing that Cleanses the Shadow of the Black Tezcatlipoca', that is to say, how to free ourselves from the prison of the First Heaven by means of the main mathematical order of the universe, and thus gain access to our light. You will also find it in this book, in Chapter 9.

Ometeotl!

7 (CHICOME)

The Dawn of the Sixth Sun

The Mexicas understood that both movement and creation occur in every single moment and realized that everything followed the same order and was created in exactly the same way.

They observed how the day took part in the four principal movements (the lunar cycle, the years, the Venus cycles and the stars and planets' cycles), and were even able to calculate with absolute accuracy the major cycles of the universe, and their effect on human behaviour.

They laid two snakes around the calendar, i.e. a rattlesnake and a red snake, to signify respectively the precession movement of the Earth's equinoxes–made up of four cycles, each lasting 6,625 years–and the revolution of our Sun around the Pleiades. As previously mentioned, they named these movements 'Suns' and noticed that they followed the same sequence of both the four 'essences', the Tezcatlipocas, and of the elements; they recounted in detail the 'chronicle' of the previous Suns and forecast the future Suns, describing what they would look like.

The Mexica calendar was carved in stone during the Fifth Sun and contains detailed information on the last five Suns. As a cyclical calendar, however, it also provides information regarding the coming Suns, in accordance with the method clearly handed down in the oral tradition.

The description of these future suns has been preserved in the memory of the guardians in the Nahuatl language–as is the case with the *Legacy*, for instance–and to this day they continue to repeat it succinctly in its oral version, making use of a series of short metaphors to describe the characteristics of each sun.

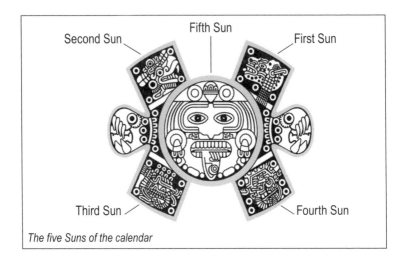

The five Suns of the calendar

The First Sun: *Ocelotonatiuh*, the 'Sun of the Jaguar'

This is the Sun of the Earth. "All was darkness and there was no movement. The *Hueyac tlacah,* the giants, were there, together with wild beasts that devoured the humans. This is how this Sun came to an end."

The jaguar is considered the main animal that inhabits the underworlds: one of these underworlds is actually known by the descriptive name of 'Wild beasts that devour humans'. The wild animals that devour human hearts in the underworlds symbolize those destructive emotions that have not been 'cleansed': from this we can therefore gather that this period was governed by shadows and dreams–the nahual–and that negative emotions were behind the extinction of the *Hueyac tlacah,* whose literal meaning is the 'big beings of the Earth', or the giants.

The Second Sun: *Ehecatonatiuh*, the 'Sun of the Wind'

"To *Ehecatonatiuh, nahui ehécatl* ('the four winds') gave direction and meaning. During this Sun, the wind carried everything away and humans were transformed into ozomahtli, 'monkeys'."

As you may recall, Ozomahtli, the monkey, is one of the glyphs in the calendar, and its distinguishing features are the blossoming of art and poetry, as well as mirth and contact with nature. From this we can gather that it must have been a period of harmonious cultural growth, while the expression 'the wind carried everything away' would suggest that this Sun ended with dreadful hurricanes.

The Third Sun: *Quiahtonatiuh*, the 'Sun of the Rain of Fire'

"In this sun there was a rain of fire and humans first became turkeys and then turned into ash."

Totolin, 'the turkey', symbolizes the ego: we therefore gather that it must have been a period of great selfishness and pride for humanity as a whole. The planet witnessed intense volcanic activity, namely a 'rain of fire'. The tale of men turning into turkeys, whose skin actually looks like it is all covered in burns, tells us of humans who were burnt and who eventually would turn into ashes.

The tradition recounts that since that time turkeys have been displaying their burnt skin, almost as a memento of that Sun, as well as a warning to prevent it ever happening again. *Nextli*, the ash, is one of the epithets[34] of the shadow, and we can thereby deduce that humans were reabsorbed into the shadow.

The Fourth Sun: *Atonatiuh*, the 'Sun of Water'

"People were not honest and the Water carried everything away." The oral tradition tells us that because human beings 'were not honest' the highest form of consciousness on the planet was the inhabitants of the seas. Going by the sentence, "the Water carried everything away", we gather that this Sun ended with a deluge.

The Fifth Sun: *Ollintonatiuh*, the 'Sun of Movement'

"It arose a long time ago. When it reaches its end, the Earth will

---

34 In this context, the term *epithet* indicates an adjective or a noun used to characterize a person or thing, like in the expression 'Catherine *the Great*'.

shake and suffering and famine will occur. Everyone will perish."

We thus gather that this sun will end with many physical earthquakes that will cause many deaths and as many individual earthquakes, which will destroy all our old structures. In this respect the oral tradition is crystal clear: *we all* will have to die; our old way of being will die and we will be forced to change. This is the Sun of solar justice.

As I have mentioned in a previous chapter, this does not mean that a new cycle begins the moment that the previous one has completely run out; there are periods of transition when the new sun slowly begins to enter the realm of its predecessor, until they both share the same level of influence. Finally we can observe that the previous Sun is exiting the stage, while handing over the baton to the new Sun for thousands of years.

What we are living through at present is the extraordinary period in which our star is reborn. In 1991, the Sixth Sun silently started to exert its influence, which on 21 December 2012 will be on a par with the influence of the Fifth Sun. We are therefore living in extraordinary times, the dawn of the Sixth Sun, which from 2021 onwards will single-handedly govern our consciousness for thousands of years.

To give it a warm welcome, in accordance with the predictions of some of the masters of the oral tradition, a ritual that belongs to this tradition will be conducted in 2021, in which thousands of people from all over the world will participate; this is a signal that over the next few years the Mexica teachings, together with their dates and predictions, will spread all over the planet.

If we want to understand what the period that spans from 2012 through to 2021 will look like, i.e. when the Fifth Sun disappears from the scene, we ought to carry out an analysis of its dualistic aspect. The Fifth Sun, the Sun of solar justice, can actually express itself in two different ways:

- *Tezcatlipoca tonatiuh,* the Sun of destruction, which creates both hurricanes and the winds that make water evaporate, the sun which warms up the Earth causing earthquakes and droughts on a collective scale, and which on an individual level creates the destructive patterns of our tonal, the waking state, and thus causes huge personal crises.

- *Quetzalcoatl tonatiuh*, the sun that is the source of life, heat and knowledge through *tzontemoc*, 'the solar fire': this is its positive influence, which on a human level makes possible the dismantling of the prison of the Moon and gives access to the positive side of the Sun, the side that leads to one's own 'blossoming'. As it is a 'Sun of justice' those who do not follow any paths of transformation shall remain stuck in the realm of Tezcatlipoca tonatiuh, and there they will face their personal and collective catastrophes; they will die and will have to face this transformation after death, when it is much more difficult to bring about, as we shall see in the chapter entitled 'Death and the Nine Underworlds'.

As the guardians of the tradition are revealing the Mexica teachings now to comply with the prophecy, the aim of this book is to share both their practical and philosophical training, so as to transform our *Yayauhqui Tezcatlipoca* shadow, the black Tezcatlipoca, towards the 'blossoming' of the many *quequetzalcoah* (in the plural) that will flower under the Sixth Sun.

The Sixth Sun: *Iztactonatiuh*, the 'White Sun'

It is not difficult to foresee what the Sixth Sun will look like, but in this respect numerology comes to our aid. Each Sun preserves the influence of its number, and presents itself on a cyclical basis: the calendar describes five of them, before starting again from number one. The Sixth Sun, therefore, will resemble the First one, although bearing the particular features of its own number, i.e. number 6. Similarly the Seventh Sun will look like the Second, the Eight like the Third, and so on, thus showing us the extent that can be reached by human consciousness and spirituality.

Number 6 directs us to the power of unified energy, and we must study this number if we want to understand what this Sun will look like and recall its name, which will be discussed later.

Number 6 tells us that this Sun facilitates the individual decision to raise *coatzin*: this is the 'venerable sexual energy' that is symbolized by a snake, and it rises through the *totonalcayo*, the seven doors of *chicomoztoc*,[35] 'the cave of power' (see figure in the colour insert); these 'doors' are energy points located in the body, and more specifically in the coccyx, the genital area, navel, chest, throat, forehead, and in the crown of the head.

On its way up, the snake activates our individual *chicomoztoc* and we go through the threshold of the unknown; the snake will come out through an ear and transform itself into a bird: a magnificent quetzal or an eagle, symbols of spiritual flight.

This means that this sun will witness the manifestation of beings who have developed extremely powerful energy handling skills, such as have never been seen before: this is what our ancestors used to call 'the return of the quequetzalcoah', hoping that many would survive the solar justice of Tezcatlipoca tonatiuh and would therefore manage to 'blossom'.

Although the Sixth Sun displays certain features that are similar to the First, these should be more accurately defined: if the Fifth Sun, for instance, was a Sun of the tonal, whose luminosity drove humankind to look externally for everything that is visible in the illusion of the day, namely in conquests and relationships, thus projecting their existence mainly outside themselves, a Sun ruled by darkness entails that the night and its forces, the dream realm (the *'unknown'*), will be the governing forces and therefore the gaze of humans will be turned inward. The Sixth Sun is a sun of the nahual: the jaguar, ruler of the underworlds, and will force people to get to know the *Chicnahumictlan*, their own underworlds, and to sort out their unconscious issues which they postponed for thousands of years.

All Suns, whether of light or of darkness, are dual: yet in the Suns of darkness dream control is not the exclusive domain of a few, but is achieved by many, which poses the risk that these people may exploit their training to keep others under their control in the daytime, having conquered them in their dreams.

The name of this sun, Iztactonatiuh, the 'white Sun', is a hint

---

35 The *chicomoztoc* is the mythical primordial cave from which everything is born, where the Aztecs used to live before the separation of their tribes. According to the oral tradition, however, on an individual level the 'cave' is our inner dimension, where the shadow takes root. The points where it is possible to go back up to the light are the energy points.

to the Seventh Heaven, the heaven of the spirit of the Moon–
which comes before all its manifestations, both on a physical and
dream level (the latter, as already explained, refers to the lunar
consciousness)–and to the Temictli, the dream world.

It is advisable to become familiar with the lunar cycles and
make the best possible use of them:

- The Moon's revolution cycle around the Earth: this is
  the sidereal cycle of 27.3 days, which resembles a 28-day
  cycle when observed from the Earth. Given that the Earth
  simultaneously moves around the Sun, for the Moon to
  go back exactly to the starting point some more time is
  required, and this is the synodic cycle of precisely 29.5
  days.

- Every 19 years the sidereal and synodic cycles happen
  to meet in the same location, thus giving rise to another
  important lunar cycle.

- We have already described how according to the quincunce and as shown in the calendar (see Figure on page
  29), the Venus and Moon cycles gather together in an
  8-year cycle.

- We have equally made reference to the number of the
  'blossoming' (13), which is based upon the movement of
  the Sun around the Pleiades.

- For a new lunar cycle to blossom, it is necessary to multiply together some of its cycles, as follows: 19 x 8 x 13,
  which results in the big lunar cycle of 1,976 years that
  underpins collective religious beliefs; the previous cycle
  started in AD 34 in the Christian era, whereas the new
  cycle started on 11 July 2010, on the day of the eclipse:
  we are therefore aware that new religious beliefs are
  becoming established and that these will rule the next
  1,976 years, although at present we do not yet know what
  these are likely to be.

The Disappearance of Time

The evolution of human consciousness has always been characterized by impressive short-lived leaps, followed by long periods of inertia: this phenomenon can easily be explained in light

of both the creation that occurs in every moment and of those forces that support the universe, together with its movement. As I have already mentioned, the four Tezcatlipocas express themselves on a spiritual, astronomical and human level, and the square that is formed by them around the cosmic cross represents both time and our Earth, whereas the inner cross stands for the movement that takes place on our planet.

The Tezcatlipocas are astronomically represented by various heavenly bodies: the black is represented by the Moon and the centre of the galaxy; the red by the *Mixcoatl*, the Milky Way, and the sunset sun; the blue by the sun at sunrise and the planet Mars, and the white by Venus and the midday sun.

These heavenly bodies have established a permanent ongoing relationship with the Earth and they are located in different positions in relation to her, on the grounds that they are the holders of time. With the alignment that is going to take place between the centre of the galaxy, the Milky Way, the Sun and Venus on 21 December 2012, the four Tezcatlipocas, the universe-sustaining forces, will be in a straight line, and the square will therefore dissolve, giving rise to the momentary disappearance of time; this process began slowly in 1991 and will reach

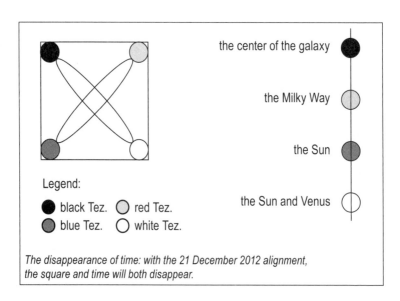

Legend:
● black Tez.   ◐ red Tez.
◉ blue Tez.   ○ white Tez.

the center of the galaxy ●
the Milky Way ◐
the Sun ◉
the Sun and Venus ○

The disappearance of time: with the 21 December 2012 alignment, the square and time will both disappear.

its peak in 2012, in conjunction with this alignment that will last just a few seconds. The tradition maintains that during these few seconds time will disappear, while a partial effect of this phenomenon will continue until the 25 December. Afterwards, as we gradually move away from the centre of the galaxy, the square of time will be formed again, and in 2021 it will newly acquire its original form.

This is why we are already experiencing events much more rapidly than ever before: the distance between thinking and its manifestation is disappearing, and a new world is being created where anything constructive or destructive tends to appear much more rapidly.

As previously mentioned, the guardians of the tradition have very meticulously inserted in the Mexica calendar the cosmic events that relate to the four essences and to the stars that represent them; similarly they have identified the dates by when our training and transformation must be completed, *if we want that our birth as Quetzalcoatl coincides with the cosmic alignment of* **21 December 2012**.

On **11 July 2010**, during the solar eclipse, the black Tezcatlipoca represented by the Moon covered the Sun, and thereby created a shadow: on that day a 'cleansing' phase of both personal and collective underworlds began, during which we can transform both our unconscious destructive shadow into a constructive one, and our yaotl, 'the enemy', astronomically represented by Saturn, into our nezahualpilli, 'the one who fasts and has overcome all his weaknesses', who is represented by Jupiter. These two heavenly bodies are both governed by the black Tezcatlipoca.

For those who have not yet begun this 'cleansing', it is better late than never. They can actually begin their training at any time, as the black Tezcatlipoca shows up every day at the darkest hour of the night, just before dawn, or at each 'black moon' listed in the calendar, which is why this training can begin either each night or whenever there is a 'black moon'.

If we understand that the universe is subject to a precise order, measure and movement, then whenever we synchronize ourselves with the relevant lunar dates, hours and phases, we will actually align our personal intention with the cosmic intelligence, which will make things easier for us. It is definitely much easier to accomplish anything when we are supported by this cosmic energy wave, rather than moving 'out of time' and ignoring its rhythms. This equates to experiencing the cosmos within ourselves.

21 December 2010, during the lunar eclipse, was the second 'date of power', the manifestation of Xipe Totec, the second Tezcatlipoca. The ordering principle gave renewed order to the dreams, thoughts, speech, emotions and actions of those who had already cleansed their shadow: this is a phase called 'sloughing', as in the case of a snake that sheds its skin, and metaphorically stands for freeing oneself from the old energies with the aim of achieving complete renewal.

As before, those who have not been able to do this at the right moment can nonetheless begin whenever they wish, in that the energy of Xipe Totec appears every day at dusk. The 'sloughing' of our old 'I' can therefore take place at any sunset, but obviously only after the shadow or the individual underworld has been cleansed.

21 December 2011, the day of the winter solstice, is the starting date of the work that is necessary to keep up this renewal, based upon the iron will of the hummingbird during the waking state (the blue Tezcatlipoca), and the unceasing activity required to come across either the hummingbird or our individual nahual in our sleep; in this way we move from our chaotic and uncontrolled sleep to the Temixoch, the 'blossomed' or lucid dreaming, and the path of nahualism.

Those who have not been able to complete their training in time, that is to say within the specified and most conducive period, can deal with this third Tezcatlipoca once their shadow has been cleansed and their old energy 'sloughed off', knowing full well that the hummingbird's energy or essence appears every day at dawn in conjunction with the sun, as well as at each winter solstice.

20 May 2012, alignment with the Pleiades, which govern the dream state: the nahual (dreaming) begins to have more power than the tonal; it is the start of the new order.

6 June 2012, the date of Quetzalcoatl and of the Sun and

Venus eclipse: Quequetzalcoah's hidden knowledge comes back to life.

On **21 December 2012**, as a result of the work carried out both during the sleep and the waking states, the energy of *coatl,* the snake, could rise inside human beings, pass through the totonalcayo (energy points, or vortexes) and transform into Quetzalcoatl.

Those who started late but have survived the destructiveness of the Fifth Sun, the so-called 'Sun of justice', will be able to discover the energy of Quetzalcoatl in any summer solstice, or in the midday sun.

A Personal Decision
Becoming a Quetzalcoatl requires a complex type of training, which is the result of a personal decision.

However, we have all carried our own Yayauhqui, our black Tezcatlipoca, since birth; the Spanish chronicles that followed the Conquest could not recognise its real nature and interpreted it through Christian filters: consequently they perceived it as a sort of demonic energy. In reality the black Tezcatlipoca is the unconscious (the shadow) and the essence of every human being, and as such it was also the main energy of ancient Mexico.

This energy can either give us everything or take everything away from us, it is either an enemy or a personal friend in either the unconscious or in the underworld, and can either lead us to our blossoming or to our destruction. If we want to succeed in becoming a Quetzalcoatl, we should start from the Tezcatlipoca, which exists as a separate entity from the Quetzalcoatl, whereas the latter cannot exist without the Tezcatlipoca, i.e. the shadow out of which light is created.

As we gradually approach this temporary disappearance of time, most of us will become aware of how much easier it will be for either fortune or misfortune to strike us, and of the amazing speed with which destructive thoughts and dreams will actually manifest themselves: in this latter phase of the sun of justice, therefore, many will experience some kind of personal catastrophe.

The reference to earthquakes and collective death at the end of this Sun is a symbolic hint at the change of all those economic, political, religious, environmental, social and psychological structures that up until now we have regarded as our foundation. This change is already underway and we will all have to change.

Those who choose to go along with this change that affects both the universe and its four columns will be able to see their creative thoughts and dreams materialize with much greater ease, and will live through a period of highly impressive evolution and transformation, which in other words could be called some genuine miracles.

Ometeotl!

*Above: details of a fresco depicting a jaguar warrior, Cacaxtla, Mexico.
Private collection photograph.*

*Below: the double-headed turquoise serpent, symbol of Ometeotl, housed in the British
Museum. 20.5 x 43.5 cm (8"x 17"), dating between 1400 and 1521.*

The chicomoztoc, from the Historia Tolteca-Chichimeca,
a 16th century Nahuatl manuscript, Bibliothèque Nationale, Paris.

The author performing a sacred ceremony.

The author performing a sacred ceremony, conducted by Xolotl, one of his masters.

Mexica-Aztec calendar: a basalt stone monolith,
weighing 25 tons, with a 3.6 meter diameter (approximately 12 ft),
housed in the Mexica room, National Museum of Anthropology, Mexico City.

8 (CHICUEY)

Ancient Trainings

How can such individual transformations occur then, practically speaking? It must be said that ancient Mexico had several methods at its disposal to bring them to fruition.

To this day the principal methods that continue to be used are the warrior dances, together with postures, obsidian mirror, breathing techniques, dream control and the temazcal bath.

The Warrior Dances

These dances reproduce the rhythm of the universe in motion, which is what we tune into. Each Tezcatlipoca features some specific dances, whose aim is to develop its characteristics; whereas other types of dances are meant to develop the qualities of various animals, and thereby bestow their powers upon the dancers. The coyote dance, for instance, bestows both sexual and magical powers; the hummingbird dance, which is danced in reverse, i.e. dancing backwards, imitating a peculiar way of flying that is sometimes practised by this bird, develops happiness and willpower; the numerous eagle dances give us the power of 'flying spiritually' (i.e. of spiritual growth), and on a deeper level give us a chance to develop the quality of 'prophetic eagle', a name reserved for the masters of the dream state. There is also the jaguar, or *ocelot*, dance, which serves to cleanse the shadow, as well as many others.

Each dance features a sequence of movements that symbolize the four elements, so that we can harmonize ourselves with them once again: circular movements represent the Wind, whereas a large forward scissor kick stands for the Fire; moving forward while dragging one's feet and zigzagging, as well as lowering the body and bowing, represent the Earth, and a forward scissor kick, but this time less vigorously, symbolizes Water.

Another typical movement is *ollin*, the cross movement, which brings us into the dynamic aspect of the universe and therefore brings about our transformation: movement means change, and dancing in this way eliminates both our obsolete structures and the resistance that we normally put up against change, and thereby we can flow in perfect unison with the universe.

In addition, these dances can be considered as preparatory exercises for nahualism, given that in this tradition the dream state masters take on animal forms during sleep: by training to do the same during the dance, we are preparing ourselves to take on an identity in the nahual.

The dance is guided by a *huehuetl*, a drum that usually follows certain patterns, rhythms and sequences based upon the number four, which symbolize the pulsations of the Earth. Sometimes these dances last for hours, and this allows the dancers to enter into an altered state of consciousness, the dreaming while awake, a trance-like state where physical limitations are transcended. Those who can make use of this state can modify their reality at will, and can, for instance, heal others or create anything that they may desire in life, because inside the circle of dancers a magnetic energy is created, which traditionally goes by the name of *chiton-tiliztli*, or 'the power of the dance'; anything that the person wishes for can thereby be invoked and drawn into his or her life.

Furthermore, there is an even deeper state called *chitontiquiza,* literally the 'power of the dance that enables the rise to the sacred level', i.e. to the higher skies where we can have prophetic or spiritual visions, or simply enter into the centeotl through a state called amomati, or 'empty mind'. What other traditions achieve through meditation is here achieved by means of these dances.

To the above list we can add the recitation of requests aimed at the wellbeing of the entire community, which makes use of magnetic energy so that the collective wellbeing is invited to come to Earth.

The whole tradition is thus summed up in these warrior dances.

The Postures

Another form of training, which also includes some elements that belong to the dance, is the training in the postures, which symbolize the essences, the Tezcatlipocas, or the animals; they either activate some specific energy points or they develop some specific skills, such as nahualism for instance. Nahualism features certain postures called *mexicatzin*, 'the venerable Mexihcah', which are synchronized with a specific number of breaths, always corresponding to those sacred numbers that belong to the cosmic mathematics that I have already explained, namely 4, 8, 9, 13, 52, 104 and 105. In this context the word 'mexihcah' refers to Metztli, the Moon, and 'venerable Mexihcah' are those who first dismantle the prison of the Moon and then develop nahualism; this training is not regarded as complete until one has acquired perfect mastery of the skills of eight animals while dreaming; and before moving on to the subsequent animal, one must have experienced all the features pertaining to the previous one. It effectively equates to leading eight lives in the nahual, while living just one in the tonal. Starting with the first animal, i.e. from stage one, one can already have access to others' dreams for the purpose of healing them: you can therefore just imagine what could be achieved in subsequent stages!

Given that this knowledge is so powerful, in that it allows one to exert one's influence over others, the mastery of dreams is clearly not the first subject that is taught. The starting point is invariably the **cleansing of one's own shadow**, as we will see in this book, so that once the power of dreams has been acquired, and in the event that one still wishes to influence someone else's dreams–which by then would no longer be a source of interest, as in the meantime we will have discovered that it is merely a waste of energy–it would be conducted exclusively and invariably in a positive sense.

The Obsidian Mirror

This is another type of training, in which the mirror enables us to see what lies beyond the tonal. The obsidian mirror is the symbol of the black Tezcatlipoca (let me remind you that *tezcatl* means 'mirror' and *poca* means 'that smokes', therefore it could be translated as the 'smoking mirror'): it may seem like a metaphor, but in this case it should be taken literally.

Through a series of rhythmic breathings based on the mathematics of 'what is known', we can reach an altered state whereby the first thing that happens when we reflect ourselves in the mirror is that our image disappears. Then some fog looms up, the same fog that we go through when we fall asleep, even though usually we fail to remember it.

The mirror is the means through which perceptions are widened, so that we enter consciously into the subtle worlds: we can then observe which type of animal we turn into in our dreams, because as we pass through the fog our face changes, and we can see the snout of an animal reflected in the mirror. Other faces can appear as well, and we can thus see who we were in our previous lives: we can heal the problems that stem from previous lives, and which are the cause of our current issues. All the faces of our shadow make an appearance and the best thing of all is that we can sow our future into its image. We can also come into contact with our ancestors and the mirror can equally be used as a source of oracular predictions.

I remember an occasion in which a European psychiatrist was taking part in one journey of initiation in Mexico. I was guiding a session of mirror exercises and the day after, during a break, she came to me and said: "Honestly speaking, I did not believe that I would disappear in the mirror and that I could see such things. I am truly impressed."

For someone who is perfectly trained, the mirror provides direct access to the level of Quetzalcoatl, but it is not so easy: the mirror must be placed inside a container full of water and we must remain in total darkness, until we manage to create some light in the mirror, so as to be able to see ourselves clearly reflected. The creation of light out of darkness is precisely the distinctive feature of the Tezcatlipoca Quetzalcoatl.

Breathing Techniques

Another easy-to-learn technique, so much so that it is explained in this book on page 99 ('The Sacred Breathing that Cleanses the

Shadow of the Black Tezcatlipoca'), makes use of highly specialized breathing exercises based on the cycles, rhythms and movements of the universe and of the sacred calendar. In compliance
with some of the clues of the prophecy, they could not be revealed
to the world any earlier than the 11 July 2010 eclipse, which is why
now is the time for them to come to light.

Dream Control

The point here is to move from temictli, or uncontrolled
dreams, where we don't have a stable and recognisable identity,
to temixoch, lucid and 'blossomed' dreaming.

To accomplish this task there are several techniques that
range from falling asleep without losing consciousness to
knowing the language of cipacnahualli, the language of 'the
unknown', or creating a dream identity that remains constant,
an 'energy double' in which we can recognise ourselves while
dreaming, and which we can use to delete our destructive
dreams and sow some constructive ones instead.

To gain access to the power of dreams, first of all we should
establish a friendly relationship with the element Fire, which
governs them; for instance, by supplying ourselves with solar
energy through some specific techniques (I will teach you one
of these in the chapter on the blue Tezcatlipoca, page 116: the
tezcatzoncatl exercise) we end up accumulating the element
Fire, as well as both the awareness and power of dreams as part
of the same process.

The Mexicas were both a lunar and solar population, and
therefore devoted a great deal of their spiritual development
to controlling their dreams, an area in which they achieved an
extraordinarily sophisticated level of knowledge.

Temazcal Bath

The Nahuatl term *temazcal* comes from *temaz*, 'steam' and
calli, 'house'.

People usually believe that the sweat lodge is reserved exclusively for healing, but it actually serves more purposes than just
this. There are many different types of sweat lodges and they
are something steeped in very rich symbolism.

The sweat lodge or 'temazcal bath'

Its shape is reminiscent of both the celestial vault and of Tonantzin's bosom (the Earth), i.e. the supreme creative forces that allow us to recreate ourselves in here and be reborn. For this reason, when leaving the lodge after some specific temazcal ceremonies, we are met by a woman, and this action symbolises this rebirth.

Some purification temazcals take place before important ceremonies, because the temazcal is also used to cleanse the shadow. Inside the lodge, because of the heat, we can have access to some altered states of consciousness that make for spiritual or prophetic visions.

The four elements are present in the temazcal, coupled with our harmony: we recite our intention over a vessel full of *Water*, and these intentions are poured together with the water over burning stones *(Earth)*, which are heated up by *Fire*; the moment that they come into contact with the water they produce the steam that symbolizes the *Wind* and that carries our intention in all directions; to ensure that this comes about, we invariably begin and conclude with the word ometeotl.

I recall a temazcal that took place before a name sowing

ceremony to disclose the possibility of a new destiny. On that particular occasion I could really see that the prophecy was manifesting through it. There were people from all over the world who consigned their intentions of a new life to the Water, all in their respective languages: English, Spanish, Polish, Nahuatl, Italian, Dutch…and although I could not really understand much of what they were saying, the energetic force that was present there was truly impressive. It was like a small-scale version of the Earth, where people would work together, bonded by a sense of brotherhood…

Ometeotl!

Yayauhqui Tezcatlipoca, the Black Tezcatlipoca: the Cleansing of the Shadow

"The I is a mere designation"
(The 14th Dalai Lama)

The cleansing of the shadow must begin by getting to know it in the first place, and by understanding the structure of our unconscious energy; in ancient times, this type of information was held exclusively by the tlamacazqui, those responsible for making offerings to Tezcatlipoca.

The following epithets of Tezcatlipoca are of particular interest, in that they provide a step-by-step description of the various facets of the darkness and of the cave, coupled with the challenges that have to be faced in order to transform the destructive shadow into its constructive equivalent:

- *Moyocoyani* is the starting point, the first reflection that appears in the mirror of creation. He who is, in and by himself. He is the essence of the individual being, the darkness from which all individual beings originate, symbolized by our image into the obsidian mirror. Our reflection's disappearance into the mirror shows us the illusion of matter. Moyocoyani is linked to the darkest hour of the night. The oral tradition says he is '*moyocoyacatzin a yac oquiyocox*', that means: 'Nobody formed him, nobody created him, he made himself, of his own will.' It is self-created creation, the being inventing himself.

- ***Yocoya*** is the idea that the individual being's essence holds about itself. The idea of a being that is about to manifest itself comes from *moyocoyani*, the darkness, and this is the first aspect that must be cleansed in our shadow. The challenge lies in understanding and accepting that human beings are simply an idea, an illusion in motion, and that the only truth is the energy of the essence, which is pure potential. As long as we are aware that this is the case, then *yocoya* (i.e. our idea of ourselves) can easily be replaced by a better idea, on the grounds that whilst we continue to have a body in the tonal we will keep up certain ideas about ourselves. The old idea will disappear the very moment our face disappears into the obsidian mirror; therefore, if we are successful in ensuring that this process is constantly repeated by using the mirror as a form of discipline, we will reach a point where these old structures will dematerialize once and for all. Another opportunity to this effect is provided by those breathing exercises by means of which we expel the old ideas that we hold about ourselves.

The Black Tezcatlipoca

- *Monenequi.* Here the literal meaning is 'the one who does what he/she likes, according to his own will'. When we analyse this process, we observe that using the idea that we have about ourselves, i.e. *yocoya*, as a starting point, we then justify our way of being in a particular way, and this then becomes the story we commit to carrying along with us, notwithstanding that it could be the source of a great deal of suffering. We persist, for example, in wanting to remain exactly the same, regardless of the perpetual movement and unaware of all the changes that occur on a constant basis; even when we are forced to renew ourselves, we end up choosing the type of experiences that resemble the same ones we have already lived through. From this tradition's standpoint, this is 'doing what one likes', meaning that we choose not to change.

- *Moquehqueloa.* This literally means 'the one who makes a mockery of us'. It is not a coincidence that in mythical tales Tezcatlipoca is constantly portrayed as the one who plays tricks and jokes at Quetzalcoatl's expense; this means that–beginning with the idea of oneself and all the stories that consequently originate from it–we start judging both ourselves and others: in other words there is a hidden part of our shadow that is busy giving rise to all our insecurities, and which plays a contributing role in creating others' insecurities too. This fake voice that inwardly attacks us is one of the most destructive aspects of our Tezcatlipoca. One of the main objectives of the mirror is to enable us to observe our own shadow: as soon as our face disappears, we can make the request to see the reflection of our moquehqueloa, and sometimes what appears is a face sporting a mocking smile, and in the meantime those unpleasant things that we keep repeating to ourselves begin to surface in our mind. This is the type of energy that must be cleansed quite urgently, either when the face disappears into the mirror or through the sacred breathing exercises.

- *Tlahnequi.* This means 'the one who has sexual desires'. This name of Tezcatlipoca follows the two preceding ones, in that sexual energy–which is creative and is the basis of self-expression–will manifest itself by generating either beauty or destruction around us, based upon the previous sequence (namely the idea that we have of ourselves, and its ensuing stories and self-judgement).

The face that we see reflected in the obsidian mirror shows us the way we express ourselves in life, i.e. either as victims or torturers, either as shy or intimidating people, as well as the way in which we express our sexuality: basically we can observe which image of ourselves we portray to the world, an image that we do not usually perceive directly, as we are not able to see ourselves.

- *Yaotl,* 'the enemy'. Unlike our current perception of the enemy as something external to us, which is the cause of all our adversities, the ancient Mexicas were well aware that the real enemy is located inside and manifests when tlahnequi, our self-expression, turns against us, and in so doing brings about illness and death.

  This is one of the most powerful experiences that we can possibly have by means of the obsidian mirror: when the reflection in our eyes is transformed and we can see in it the resentment that almost all of us feel towards ourselves, we then realize that if this image–which is definitely part of ourselves–could jump out of the mirror, it would actually assault us. *The main goal of the cleansing of the shadow is the transformation of this enemy into a friend.*

- *Necoc yaotl*, 'the mutual enemy'. To understand what necoc yaotl is we need to know how the ancient Mexicas used to view war. They used to say that for a war to break out–ranging from a mere dispute between two people to conflicts affecting several nations and their respective populations–it was not enough for the yaotl, one's own enemy, to urge the destruction of the other side, but that equally the other's yaotl would in turn react by unleashing its anger, its own desire to destroy us, because one enemy alone is not enough to wage war: it must find a response that originates from the other side's inner enemy. The necoc yaotl is the part of our shadow that drives us towards being aggressive with others, what instigates conflicts among people, families and nations alike, which is why Tezcatlipoca was referred to as 'the one that leads you to either war or peace'. The conquistadors regarded it as the devil itself, although Tezcatlipoca is actually none other than ourselves. In the mirror we see the reflection of our own aggression towards the outside world, which will eventually turn against us, as a great deal of our energy is dispersed when we are involved in conflictual situations.

• *Telpochtli,* 'the one who falls and makes us fall over weaknesses'. In ancient times, those who trained to be in charge of the offerings to Tezcatlipoca were carefully monitored to identify their specific weak points, which could range from belligerence to sexuality or perhaps self-complacency, or maybe the passion for too much food. Then, at the right moment and being careful that they would not notice, they would find themselves at the receiving end of certain temptations: if they fell for them, they would consequently be expelled from the path of the offering of the force on the grounds that they were totally controlled by the shadow instead of being able to control it. The telpochtli is that part of us which invariably falls prey to our main weaknesses, the part that in this eternal renewal process prevents us from gaining access to a new idea of ourselves and to its manifestation.

In the obsidian mirror at this stage there usually appears a very weak and fearful reflection, devoid of strength; sometimes it resembles a child, and this is a clear expression of our fragility and lack of willpower.

• *Titlacahuan* is 'the other [I] of the heart', the source of all feelings. In the oral tradition this type of information is codified as 'he who can see', and the sentence associated to this epithet is: "We are like him. He looks at us with our very own eyes." Once we have managed to overcome our weaknesses, we are sufficiently strong to be able to see what we really are, without being afraid of it. We can see both our light and our darkness, together with our dualistic aspects: we can come to terms with them all and be able to control them at will. Reaching this stage means that we have already done a great deal of cleaning of our 'cave' and we can now start observing our reflection in the mirror without judging or mocking it, and devoid of aggression. Now we can really see ourselves.

- **Chalchiuhtotolin,** literally 'the jade turkey'. The prancing about of the turkey turns it into the symbol of ego and vanity and given that traditionally jade was regarded as the most precious stone in ancient Mexico, the jade turkey symbolizes the vanity of all vanities. For someone who has not cleansed his shadow and happens to be a highly successful person, or rich or beautiful, or all three, the turkey represents one of the worst traps devised by the moquehqueloa, who makes a mockery of him by cajoling him into believing that he is superior to everyone else. It is however no more than an illusion brought about by the concepts that we have about ourselves, and falling into this trap is often the source of a great deal of suffering. This kind of trap is even worse if those who fall into it have embarked upon a spiritual path, as these people tend to be more aware and therefore turn their minor or major successes into fuel for the ego. This is why at this stage people do not usually talk about the type of reflection that they see in the mirror... it is no coincidence that in mythical tales the turkey is the third nahual animal of Tezcatlipoca: its task is to alert the masters of the dream state so that they do not fall into the extreme of the ego and they do not dominate others through the sleep state.

- *Tezcatlipoca tonatiuh,* 'the sun of destruction'. These are all those destructive types of behaviour produced by the ego, which find their expression in the tonal; the cleansing of the shadow enables us to overcome all the distinct forms in which Tezcatlipoca has manifest previously in our lives: this is how we can transcend the sun of destruction, and thereby bring to an end the various facets of this destructive shadow, which then transforms into the highest aspects of the unconscious, into the highest and most beneficial expressions of the black Tezcatlipoca. This is a state of transition, which appears invisible in the obsidian mirror.

- *Nezahualpilli*, 'the one who fasts'. Fasting plays an important role in ancient Toltec and Mexica training: its purpose is to weaken the tonal and strengthen the nahual, to the point that the nahual can feed the tonal, making it even stronger than before. Not only does it mean that we are no longer dependent on food, but also that we have been able to withstand our temptations and have overcome our personal weaknesses, and consequently that we have managed to achieve an impeccable level of discipline and have transcended our self-destruction. Now the face that we see reflected in the mirror is the face of a person at peace with himself, who possesses a much deeper gaze, the gaze of a 'man of knowledge'.

- *Ixnextli* is one of the female names of Tezcatlipoca, which literally means 'she whose head is covered in ash'. In ancient rituals, those who had been initiated to the knowledge of Tezcatlipoca would cover their entire bodies in ash in order to transcend the illusion of the physical form, and to discover and see only and exclusively the essence of individual beings, only and exclusively beauty in the darkness, in the nothingness and in the All. This is a higher state of consciousness and perception, which leads us to transcend all forms of judgement, guiding us to see the truth.

  Now in the mirror there is nothing but darkness. At the beginning of the practice we similarly noticed that our face was disappearing, something which made us drop all concepts that we had about ourselves, but here and now the darkness in the mirror has evolved: this equates to seeing reality beyond form. If we continue to use the mirror, the only thing that it will show us will be the essence of our individual being, the darkness of moyocoyani.

- *Ixquimilli*, 'the one who fasts and covers his eyes'. Tezcatlipoca is often shown with blindfolded eyes to signify that he has overcome the illusion of the external material world and that he is developing his inner vision coupled with spiritual vision and other sensations: this is why he follows the right path, equipped with his inner vision of both dream and dreaming while awake (a kind of trance) states.

- *Ixcuinan*, is another female name of Tezcatlipoca, whose meaning is 'the mother who protects the face'. This is the maternal instinct to protect one's children, namely the development of their identity (the face): it is a quality that is ascribed to Mother Earth and that is embodied by the Moon.

- *Oztoteotl*, 'the Lord of the caves': this is the name of the essence or energy that rules inside the caves. For those who have been initiated this means being the master of one's own cave, of one's own chicomoztoc, or darkness, the location of the seven doors (or energy points) called totonalcayo (the equivalent of chakras), which can be crossed to find light at the exit of the cave, moving from Tezcatlipoca to Quetzalcoatl.

- *Tepeyolohtli*, 'the Lord of the heart of mountains'. 'Heart of mountains' refers to those caves that lie deep inside sacred mountains. As is the case in many other ancient traditions, in the Toltec-Mexica tradition it is very important to climb to such locations to give some order to the chaos that rules further below. Once we have become the masters of our own cave, we can move to the next level up, the level of 'guardian of the mountain', who is equipped with sufficient energy to rule its heart and is able to influence from there the collective destiny of the surrounding area. In today's Mexico such guardians do actually still exist, although they keep themselves well hidden; they are known by the name of *tepeyolotl* and are the supreme exponents of the development of the black Tezcatlipoca, having tamed not just their own shadow, but being capable of cleansing even the collective shadow of an entire region.

- *Metztli*, another female name for the black Tezcatlipoca: this is the Moon, which governs both the dream state and the nahual. The challenge in this case lies in eliminating the destructive force that she creates while we dream and taking control of our dreams to transform them, thus exerting our creative will both in the dream and in the waking state, in the tonal as much as in the nahual.

EXERCISE

The Sacred Breathing that Cleanses the Shadow of the Black Tezcatlipoca

At this stage I would like to remind you of the meaning of some secret numbers, so that you can understand clearly how the sacred breathing cleanses the shadow, the purpose of which is the realization of everything that lies along the path of Quetzalcoatl.

- **13:** the number of the 'blossoming' and of solar change.
- **8:** the Venus-Moon cycle that rules both dreams and the complementary duality of Xolotl-Quetzalcoatl, shadow-light.
- **9:** the number of the shadow, of the underworlds.
- **104:** from the Earth's standpoint, 104 years are necessary for the cosmos (using Venus as the reference point) to return to its original position and give rise to a new cycle.

Method

Keep your eyes closed while breathing, inhale through the nose and mentally count up to 13 at your own pace; the intention is to inhale the Sun's therapeutic power, the cosmic order with its sacred mathematics, and the transforming solar power that is connected to the number 13.

Exhale through the mouth, mentally counting up to 9, at the same pace that you used when inhaling; in addition to the air, we also exhale the energy of that particular aspect of the shadow from which we want to free ourselves.

Inhaling while counting to 13 and exhaling while counting to 9 represent one entire breathing cycle; 13 cycles like this equate to completing one 'movement'.

In total there are 8 movements, that is to say 104 breathing cycles, by means of which our energy will become aligned with the cosmos.

Between one movement and the next there is a pause, which is used to give an intention to the movement that is underway. This intention is always in harmony with the meaning of each of the numbers, as you can see in Chapter 5, 'The Mathematical Language of 'What is Known' (the Tonal).

Given that this breathing exercise symbolizes the passage from the shadow (represented by the numbers 9 and 8) to the light (represented by the number 13), the most auspicious time to do this is at dawn, and the direction to be facing is East, which is the direction of the Sun. A very auspicious day to start the training is the day of the 'black moon', i.e. the day before a new moon.

These 8 movements make up the daily exercise, which is to be repeated for 13 consecutive days without interruption, and followed by 8 rest days, thus totalling 21 days.

This 21-day cycle will have to be repeated 8 times in order to complete the first cleansing of the shadow; in the course of our life we ought to cleanse the shadow at least 4 times.

There are people who have acquired the habit of doing this every year; once they become aware of the level of transformation that it brings about, many decide to adopt it as their regular practice throughout their entire life.

To begin with, find a comfortable position and face the East.

Ce Ollin, first movement.

While mentally counting to 13, inhale the therapeutic power of the Sun, the force of change.

While mentally counting to 9, exhale your yocoya, the old concept that you have of yourself, willing yourself to become free from it.

Repeat this breathing cycle in its entirety 13 times.

At the end, issue the command that corresponds to this movement:

> *"Ce ollin, first movement: I establish the intention of cleansing my shadow inside the mind of the universe, which is what gives life, measure and movement. The energy and rhythm of the universe become synchronized to fully heal my destructive side, the old idea I had about myself."*

Wait for a short while, until you feel or have a sense that the energy has achieved its task.

Ome Ollin, second movement.

While mentally counting to 13, inhale the therapeutic power of the Sun, the force of change.

While mentally counting to 9, exhale your monenequi (the energy of your past based upon the story that you have created by yourself to justify your resistance to change) and your suffering, in order to free yourself completely from such energy. Fully exhale the energy of your own history.

Repeat this breathing cycle in its entirety 13 times.

At the end, issue the command that corresponds to this movement:

> *"Ome ollin, second movement: I ask that the energy of the universe descend through my body either like a snake (the ancestral therapeutic symbol) or in a snake-like movement, and thus erase from my bones my own personal story and similarly erase it from the energy of my ancestors, so as to heal them too."*

Wait for a short while, until you feel or have a sense that the energy has achieved its task.

Yei Ollin, third movement.

While mentally counting to 13, inhale the therapeutic power of the Sun, the force of change.

While mentally counting to 9, exhale your moquequehloa, that part of your shadow that mocks you and gives rise to your insecurities. Exhale that inner voice that attacks you.

Repeat this breathing cycle in its entirety 13 times.

At the end, issue the command that corresponds to this movement:

> *"Yei ollin, third movement: I ask that the power of the Sun descend into my body and reach my blood, which transforms into a snake of energy that goes through all my organs and systems and heals them. My blood becomes both my medicine and my family's medicine too, by virtue of the blood connection that exists between us."*

Keep making this energy flow into your bloodstream until you feel that all your organs have been fully healed.

Nahui Ollin, fourth movement.

While mentally counting to 13, inhale the therapeutic power of the Sun, the force of change.

While mentally counting to 9, exhale your tlahnequi, all the imbalanced sexual energy that causes your self-destructive expressions.

Repeat this breathing cycle in its entirety 13 times.

At the end, issue the command that corresponds to this movement:

> *"Nahui ollin, fourth movement: I ask for the descent of energy in the shape of a fire snake, so that it takes away any sexual misconduct of mine, all the negative energy that I have created in my sleep and which is now accumulated in my body, and all the destructive dreams that I have created which are currently driving me towards my self-destruction."*

Now visualize a new dream: you are going for a walk, for instance, and while walking you stumble across an object that is very precious to you. Give this object a precise meaning, such as your own healing or anything that you may really need. In your visualization, grab a hold of this object.

Now transform this whole visualization into a snake made of energy, which descends and goes through your whole body, and entrust your visualization to the Earth: in this way you will have sown your dream, by planting it into the earth.

Subsequently, come back to yourself and give yourself the command to repeat the same dream over the next few days; when this materialises, it will be a sign indicating that it will come true in the reality of the waking state, and it will manifest even if you have forgotten your dream.

Wait a while, until you feel or have a sense that the energy has achieved its task.

Mahcuilli Ollin, fifth movement.
While mentally counting to 13, inhale the therapeutic power of the Sun, the force of change.

While mentally counting to 9, exhale your yaotl, your inner enemy, your own self-destructive force.

Repeat this breathing cycle in its entirety 13 times.

At the end, point your fingers towards the Earth and issue the command that corresponds to this movement:

> *"Mahcuilli ollin, fifth movement: through my fingers I*

receive the energy of the Earth, together with all her heal-
ing power and all her strength."

Once you feel you have stored up sufficient power, join your palms together, preferably in front of your chest, and direct the energy by means of the intention: may it heal your inner organs, may it cleanse your shadow or may it bathe you in the river of the Earth's abundance. This form of healing is the work of Tonantzin, our Mother Earth, and therefore transcends your personal limitations.

Wait a while, until you feel or have a sense that the energy has achieved its task.

Chicoacen Ollin, sixth movement.

While mentally counting to 13, inhale the therapeutic power of the Sun, the force of change.

While mentally counting to 9, exhale your necoc yaotl, that part of yourself that causes you to be in conflict with many people. Free yourself of all the anger and resentment that you feel towards a particular individual or in general.

Repeat this breathing cycle in its entirety 13 times.

At the end, issue the command that corresponds to this movement:

"Chicoacen ollin, sixth movement: I ask that the rhythm
of the universe (which is expressed by the numbers 6,625,
260, 104, 52, 13, 9, 8, 4, 2 and 1) descend in a downward
spiral movement from the cosmos down to me, bringing
back and reconciling all my energy with the harmonious
measure and movement of the universe. Furthermore,
I ask that every organ in my body, every relationship
or any other aspect of my life may tune into the correct
rhythm of the universe."

Wait a while, until you feel or have a sense that the energy has achieved its task.

Chicome Ollin, seventh movement.

While mentally counting to 13, inhale the therapeutic power of the Sun, the force of change.

While mentally counting to 9, exhale your Tezcatlipoca tonatiuh, all the

destructive aspects of the tonal, the waking state.
Repeat this breathing cycle in its entirety 13 times.
At the end, issue the command that corresponds to this movement:

> *"Chicome ollin, seventh movement: I ask that ometeotl, the dualistic and complementary energy, become one in order to create what I desire."*

This energy manifests as two snakes, one that comes from the North and the other from the South. Unite them above your head: they become one single snake that descends through your body until it reaches the Earth, and this is how you sow your dream into her.

You can 'sow your dream' 1, 2, 4 or 7 times, depending on how many things you need, remembering however to always sow your request when this snake-like energy is descending.
Wait a while, until you feel or have a sense that the energy has achieved its task.

Chicuey Ollin, eighth movement.

While mentally counting to 13, inhale the therapeutic power of the Sun, the force of change.
While mentally counting to 9, exhale your chalchuihtotolin, your ego.
Repeat this breathing cycle in its entirety 13 times.
At the end, issue the command that corresponds to this movement:

> *"Chicuey ollin, eighth movement. I ask that from the 8 corners of the universe the cosmic energy comes and reaches my heart, so that my shadow can reach both nezahualpilli to overcome my weaknesses and oztoteotl to transform me into the master of my cave, having defeated the destructive aspect of my darkness."*

Joining your palms together–which is the physical symbol of ometeotl–wait a while, until you feel or have a sense that the energy has achieved its task.
At the end, repeat the word *Ometeotl* 4 times.

Sometimes beginners may be carried away by the fact that they have to count, or may find it difficult to concentrate on the particular state that they wish to reach, if at the same time they also need to keep track of the number of breathing repetitions. If you feel the need to be guided through these breathing exercises, you are welcome to download, completely free of charge, a video using the following link:

http://www.blossomingbooks.com/en/books/thedawn.html

Ometeotl!

Xipe Totec, the Red Tezcatlipoca: the Renewal

Xipe Totec, literally 'our Lord of sloughing', 'the one who sheds his skin' is the second Tezcatlipoca, the *tlatlauhqui* ('red') and the one who ensures that movement is constant and that pushes us to change. According to the tradition, Xipe Totec, or Xipe, as he is affectionately nicknamed, would skin himself each evening so that the Sun could be dyed with the red of his own blood, when at sunset in the West the star makes the Earth pregnant to ensure that a new day follows the night.

For this reason Xipe Totec appears in the Códices with the skin of his hands just hanging off, after he has skinned himself; the conquistadors interpreted all this very literally and became convinced that these images portrayed a practice in which people were actually skinned, whereas in fact they relate to one of the four creative forces of the universe: this is the force that each spring is

Xipe Totec

behind the Earth's renewal, and which renews us at every moment within the framework of the only reality that exists in the universe, i.e. movement.

During the ritual New Year dances–celebrated on 12 March–Xipe Totec is always portrayed as an old man dancing with an old woman (his complementary aspect), and together they symbolize the year that has just gone by. Then the *'sahumadoras'*, the women who burn an aromatic resin called copal, generate a cloud of smoke out of which comes a young Xipe Totec coupled with *Xochiquetzalli*, i.e. his complementary aspect, a young woman who symbolizes the Earth, and who will be symbolically made pregnant by Xipe to give birth to the forthcoming new year.

Xipe governs the red sky, and is the one who gives order to every aspect of creation, from the cosmos down to the Earth.

Tlatlauhqui more accurately means 'what shines and becomes red', and tradition defines him as: 'He who designates and governs the cosmic order; he gives order to the ideas that emerge from the darkness'.

He manifests as Quetzalcoatl's father, *Mixcoatl*, 'the cloudy snake' of the Milky Way, also called 'the star and dawn hunter'.

Those responsible for making offerings to Xipe Totec were called 'sky readers': for their astronomical observations they would use a pair of sticks with a hole in the middle, which defined the position of a particular star in relation to another. Thanks to their extensive knowledge of the energies they were able to calculate the effect that particular star would have on the Earth, from its specific position. Such knowledge continues to exist nowadays, even though it is kept hidden.

Xipe Totec too is endowed with several epithets:
- *Mixcoatl*, 'the cloudy snake' (the Milky Way).
- *Xiuhcóatl*, 'the fire snake', which governs renewal in dreams, what tradition refers to as 'red dream'.
- *Camaztli*, 'the renewal hunter by means of the breath': a substantial part of the message contained in the book that you hold in your hands refers to this name, namely the possibility of attaining a new life, using renewal as the starting point, and thus 'hunt' yourself, in the sense of taming yourself.

- *Itztlapaltotec*, 'the Lord of the red obsidian'. There are some red obsidian mirrors whose purpose is not the reflection of what is not evident, as is the case for the black mirror, but are rather used as a means through which we can create reality.

- *Chicahuaztli*, 'the one who leaves his strength inside the Earth for her renewal': in the dances Xipe Totec is often portrayed by using straight lines painted on the body of the dancers, which symbolize the grooves with which soil is marked in anticipation of its subsequent sowing and future harvest.

EXERCISE

Breathing Exercise for Renewal
through the Essence, or Energy, of Xipe Totec

The number of both creation and renewal is the number 7.
The type of breathings contained in this exercise will induce some altered states of consciousness, which allow our reflection to be seen either in the obsidian mirror, or inside a black bowl full of water, or even in the waters of a flowing river.

Method
With one of these tools that enable you to see your reflection, turn preferably towards the West, the direction of Xipe Totec.
Keep your eyes closed while you breathe.
Inhale through the nose and mentally count up to 7 at your own pace; your intention is to inhale the renewing power of the universe.
Exhale through the mouth, mentally counting up to 7, at the same pace used for inhaling; when you exhale, exhale your resistance to change along with the air.

This equates to completing one full breathing cycle.
7 cycles like this make up a 'movement'; there are 4 movements altogether, that is to say 28 breathings, which will tune you into the energy

of renewal, in a semi-altered state of perception.

Once the four movements have been completed, open your eyes either in front of the mirror, or in front of the water; notice your reflection, then immediately close your eyes again. Open them again, but this time narrowly, relax your gaze as if slightly blurred and start to use your lateral, or peripheral vision: try to see your current face reflected in this way, without focusing too sharply on it. Your face will tend to disappear, to become dimmer: when you have managed to make it disappear–for some this may happen on day one, whereas others may need to try many, many times–ask the reflection to show you your future face when you have grown old, after many years have gone by. Those wrinkles that you see in the reflection symbolize the grooves of the Earth, to signify that you have spent time on Earth and have accrued some experience in the process.

Give a specific intention to each wrinkle: for instance, this particular wrinkle signifies all the journeys that you have embarked upon; that one the wise person that you have managed to transform yourself into, and so on and so forth.

By assigning a specific intention to each wrinkle you will be able to create the type of life that you would like to lead today; when you then return to the present, your energy will have been codified so that your future may follow precisely the same instructions that you have just drawn upon the water, or in the mirror. You will have created a destiny in your face.

If you turn this exercise into a form of at least weekly discipline, based upon the mathematical pattern of the number 7, you will shape the course of your life: you will be the one to draw those grooves on the ground, instead of allowing your life, together with your unconscious, or your shadow, to become your creator.

Ometeotl!

Huitzilopochtli, the Blue Tezcatlipoca: Sustaining the Change

Once this renewal has taken place, the next step in the cosmic cross is to sustain this change and transform it into a new life; to this end both willpower and discipline are required, as they enable us to continue to pursue this idea.

Huitzilopochtli means several different things, but its most well-known and widespread interpretations have ended up being significantly distorted, so much so that they describe him as the essence or energy of war, to whom they would dedicate many sacrificial offerings.

At this stage, I think it is important to go back to the legend that describes his birth: *Tonantzin Coatlicue,* Mother Earth, was busy cleaning when a force in the shape of a feather entered her: at that very moment she became aware that she was pregnant with a special being, Huitzilopochtli. Tonantzin Coatlicue kept her pregnancy hidden, but her daughter *Coyolxauhqui,* the Moon, became aware of it and flew into a rage; and she and her other sisters, the stars of the South, tried to interrupt her pregnancy.

Inside his mother's womb, Huitzilopochtli, told her not to worry and Tonantzin went to *Coatepec*, the Snake Mountain, where she gave birth to Huitzilopochtli, the warrior, who, heavily armed, fought a ferocious battle with Coyolxauhqui and cut her into pieces, which is why the Moon has different phases. After witnessing the outcome of the battle, the other sisters fled towards the South to avoid crossing the path of the rising Sun, Huitzilopochtli.

This legend is a metaphor full of hidden meaning, which I have already mentioned: based upon their understanding of the First Heaven, Mexicas and Toltecs developed their knowledge of the different lunar phases and of their influence on the Earth, coupled with a method whereby they could make use of them to destroy the prison of the Moon and therefore elevate themselves above duality. This is why in the main ancient temple of Tenochtitlan there is a stone sculpture portraying the Moon 'cut into pieces' at the foot of the temple of Huitzilopochtli, the Sun at dawn that every day defeats the Moon, and which signifies the highest spiritual achievement: to transcend the First Heaven, defeat the Moon and unite with the Sun.

Coyolxauhqui, the moon 'cut into pieces': stone sculpture discovered inside Tenochtitlan's 'Templo Mayor' (main temple), in present-day Mexico City.

The dismembered Moon dropped at the feet of the Sun symbolized the order of the Fifth Sun, the 'solar justice', which was then fully in charge, and which was presided over by the energies of the day.

Huitzilopochtli

From 2012, and especially from 2021, this order will change and the energies of the night–the nahual, the Moon and the stars–will gain the upper hand, and this will be accompanied by a momentous change in global consciousness.

The word *Huitzilin* has several meanings. It is the hummingbird, a tiny bird that can fly even though its wings are so short that flying should be impossible from a purely aerodynamic standpoint. This is why it is considered the 'bird of the impossible', the energy that can make us overcome all sorts of difficulties. Ancient tradition says that the hummingbird is the only bird capable of defeating the eagle: aware of the phenomenal sharpness of the eagle's eyesight, the hummingbird pecks at the eagle's eyes and thus blinds it. It is also the only bird capable of flying backwards, the type of flight that is imitated during the 'dance of the hummingbird' and whose purpose is to evoke in us the same powers that it possesses: the power of discipline and willpower, to be able to do anything we wish in our life.

There is also another root *huitztli*, which means 'thorn', as this essence or energy has the power and the strength to withstand all the difficulties encountered along the path. This is the same strength with which the Mexicas were endowed, which allowed them to eliminate all the obstacles they had to face along their path.

In the cipacnahualli, the language of 'the unknown', the hummingbird plays a vital role, in that it is the animal that appears in prophetic visions, both in those that occur during the ensoñación (the dream while awake state) and in those generated during lucid dreaming, when we have the vision of a hummingbird–usually moving leftwards (which is why it is called 'the hummingbird that flies to the left') and blue in colour–and we follow it, we pass through some blue fog and we enter directly into the future.

Huitzilopochtli too has various names:

- **Tetzahuitl**, 'the soothsayer' or 'fortune teller'. When we are able to overcome our limitations, we manage to do some amazing things, such as displaying the gift of prophetic speech, divination and oracular predictions. One of the simplest ways to begin to develop such skills is by observing the hummingbird in the tonal: if it flies around in circles, that is considered an auspicious sign, whereas if it hangs upside down and appears so still it seems frozen, that means that some misfortune will occur somewhere, or that death may strike. Another method consists in making use of the obsidian mirror, through which those who have been trained can go beyond the blue fog of their dreams, and proceed to see the future.

  The third method consists in meeting 'the hummingbird that flies to the left' while dreaming, and the Huitzilopochtli exercise at the end of this section will explain how to go about that.

- **Cuauhtlahteotl**, 'the family tree': while dreaming the hummingbird can also take us to our ancestors' world and thus enable us to discover our cuauhtlahteotl.

- **Painalli**, literally 'the one who runs fast', a synonym of 'movement'. This essence or energy facilitates a more rapid change and is associated with the planet Mercury, which in this tradition bears this very name.

EXERCISE

Huitzilopochtli

This is a Mexica exercise that aims to invite this essence into our life so that we can recover our discipline in the tonal, and develop the gift of making prophecies in the nahual. This exercise is to be performed only at sunrise.

Method

Go to a place where you can see the sunrise, which symbolizes the 'hummingbird that flies to the left'. Communicate with it by simply formulating the intention of recovering your discipline and willpower and of seeing the hummingbird while dreaming, so that you are able to follow it until you receive some prophetic powers from it.

Look directly at the sun for a few moments, then utter a loud: "*Xihualhui!*",[36] which means 'come' in ancient Nahuatl.

Close your eyes and you will see a small electric blue dot moving quickly to your left. This is the Sun that in the nahual is transforming into a hummingbird. Repeat this at least four times, and each time the shape of the small dot will become clearer, until it takes on the outline of a hummingbird.

If you are truly disciplined and turn this exercise into your daily practice, within a short period of time the Sun will restore your will and the hummingbird will start to appear to you in your dreams: at this stage be sure to follow it immediately, as it will lead you into the future, once you have gone through either the blue fog or the blue light.

How to Recover the Lost Energy

The appearance of the hummingbird in our dreams is of little

---

36 Pronounced: 'shewalwe' (translator's note).

value to us if we do not remember anything afterwards. Recalling one's dreams requires the type of energy that we have usually lost, owing to relationships, sexuality, work…, and so on.

The most significant and representative exercise of ancient Mexico, so much so that it was immortalized in stone sculptures in almost every sacred site, is what the Mayans used to call *chac mool*, 'rain bowl', which in Nahuatl bears the name of *tezcatzoncatl*, 'the group of those who know the mirror'.

Its purpose is to recover the energy that was lost and to return whatever energy others had 'deposited' in us; in the course of sexual relationships, for instance, each partner leaves some energy inside the other partner. The same thing happens when we are in conflict with someone: both parties involved lose some of their energy, which is 'deposited' in the other. The same thing occurs when we fall in love, or in the relationship between master and disciple, or again in the various stages and locations that we go through in our life, and so on.

In every type of relationship there are energy exchanges, and this breathing exercise enables us to recover the energy that we have left in others and give back the energy that others have left in us. The result is that our tonal is lightened and we strengthen our nahual, from which we derive the highest level of strength that we can use to remember our dreams and to modify our old patterns while dreaming.

EXERCISE

Tezcatzoncatl

Method
At night, before falling asleep, assume the posture of tezcatzoncatl, as shown by the picture on your right. Align yourselves along the East-West axis, with your head towards the East. Start the exercise with your head facing left. Both thumbs and index fingers form a circle around the navel, which—as you may recall—is the location of the nahual during our waking state.

While inhaling through the nose, mentally formulate the intention of drawing to yourselves all the energy that you have left in others; then slowly exhale through the mouth while turning your head to the right, thus giving back the energy that others have left in you.
Count this as your first breathing repetition.

Now with your head turned to the right, as you can see in the statue in this picture below, inhale through the nose, again drawing the energy to yourself; then while exhaling through the mouth, turn your head to the left, and give back the energy that was 'deposited' inside.
This counts as another breathing repetition.

Continue like this, alternating the breathing reps first with your head turned to the right and then to the left, until you will have counted 13 of them (i.e. 7 to the left and 6 to the right).

This figure is a chac mool, *which in the Mayan language means 'rain bowl' (the one that he holds in his hands), whereas those statues that hold an obsidian mirror in their hands are called* tezcatzoncatl, *'the group of those who know the mirror'.*
These statues were built to show people how to do the corresponding exercises, resembling in this respect the function of yoga positions. Beginners would simply practise by forming a ring with their fingers around their navel, whereas slightly more advanced practitioners would use the water bowl, whilst experts would use the mirror.

Now rest for a short while, then repeat this cycle of 13.
Now rest again for another short while, then repeat the cycle of 13 a third time.

After another short rest, repeat the cycle a fourth time to reach 52 breathing repetitions altogether, i.e., the number of the New Fire, which equates to a new dream.

At the end either utter or mentally reflect upon your intention, which is to become a dream warrior and to recall your dreams. Tell your nahual that if it were to see the hummingbird it should then follow it, and both of them would thereby go through the blue fog that only the prophets have managed to cross.

Ometeotl!

12 (MAHTLACTLI OMOME)

Death and the Nine Underworlds

"The only certainty in this life is death"
(Mexican proverb)

Our concept of 'enlightenment' at the end of this cycle on Earth is to merge with the Sun and live life from its higher perspective in a state of unity and in interaction with the universe: at death one can reach the Sun by exiting the body through the heart. For the most spiritually ambitious, 'enlightenment' equates to learning to die by exiting through the crown of the head, thus creating an 'energy double' that possesses a permanent individuality, and which is in complete control while constantly journeying between physical and subtle universes. A sage of this stature is called 'nahual', as in the case of the dream consciousness, because he or she has attained such perfect mastery of this state that his or her energy double can interact with the waking state.

As already mentioned, according to the ancient Toltec-Mexica tradition, we come to this world equipped with a fixed amount of energy; if this energy is fully used up before we have been able to adequately unburden ourselves on an emotional level, and before we have become wise enough to be able to die exiting through the heart, we will find ourselves in the Mictlan, the 'place of the dead'. Here we will be given a final opportunity to resolve the problem, and some time in which to do it. If we were to fail, however, all our individual experiences, our memory and reminiscences would be erased, and this would turn into real torment for us. All that would be left of us would go to the centeotl, the primordial energy, where it may lie dormant for a long time, or it may become involved in another creative phase, which however would have nothing to do with us. It would turn into something else, whereas we would disappear, 'erased from the game'. If, however, we seize the opportunities provided by the underworlds (as we shall see further on), and overcome the difficult trials of the first eight underworlds one after the other, we will reach the ninth, where our eternal rest lies. Unlike the previous case, where the centeotl energy may well be resting but we as individuals will have disappeared, here it is *us* who can actually rest; and we can choose whether we want to do so for ever, or whether to return to Earth with a renewed teyolia, to have another attempt at following the spiritual path that leads to the great death, to the union with the Sun.

To avoid having to face the underworlds–which, as we shall see, is a long and painful process–the future 'men and women of knowledge' were taught since childhood to perform the 'small death' exercise before going to sleep. They would slightly open the energies located between the navel and the heart, and in this way they would train to do the same at the moment of death; this would allow them to leave the body by exiting through the chest, like butterflies or hummingbirds, and to become united directly with the Sun, or to rise even further above. Very few traditions can offer the individual such a level of choice, i.e., whether through one's death to subscribe or not, as the case may be, to this collective path that was outlined earlier. As far as the training towards such a decision is concerned, it is important to experience unity in this life, and to ask ourselves whether we are willing to remain in this unity forever.

If we discover that we do not want to do so, we will require some further specialized training to die an even higher death: in this case we would exit the body through the crown of the head, and subsequently we would remain in a state of permanent individuality.

The rationale behind the appearance of this information in Chapter 12 is that in the mathematics of 'what is known' (of the tonal), the number 12 means to see clearly all that was hidden, and death has always been one of the most stimulating mysteries for humankind.

A very popular Mexican proverb says: "The only certainty in this life is death", which shows the kind of simple and direct relationship that Mexicans have with death to this day.

Mexico is famous for its annual festivity that commemorates the dead, which for us is the most important event of the whole year: the altars, the colours, the invitation that is extended to our ancestors to come back for one day to enjoy their favourite delicacies. This festivity lasts for three days, a European legacy that stems from pagan celebrations; in reality, the ancient Mexica calendar would reserve as much as three 'scores', i.e., 60 days, to the subject of death. This was the time when they would talk about the 'great' death and how to prepare for it; the time when contact was established with dead ancestors, warriors and sages who had crossed the threshold, or had simply come back to life in a different guise, in a different form of existence; and so, instead of fearing death, the Mexicas would make collective preparations for it.

Those who are unable to become 'men and women of knowledge' and thus transcend the first three Tezcatlipocas will experience a type of death that is completely different from those who have managed to reach one of the levels, or degrees, of Quetzalcoatl; it is therefore advisable to be well aware of the various types of death and train accordingly.

In the years to come, the Fifth Sun (Tecpatl Tonatiuh, the Sun of justice) will exert an intense influence as it reaches the end of its reign, which will occur between 2013 and 2021. Movement, or change, is inevitable: whoever opposes it by opting to remain loyal to their old structures, *will nonetheless be forced to change anyway, due to the action of the last great change: death. In other words, the choice lies between movement and death.*

We need not be afraid, however: we must simply seize this opportunity for change, and do it together with the universe, the Sun and the Earth. The sheer amount and depth of information that the Mexicas held on *Miquiztli*, or 'death' in ancient Nahuatl, makes up one of the most important receptacles of thanatological knowledge of the entire ancient world. Miquiztli is one of the 20 glyphs along the calendrical wheel, and those born under this sign will find themselves in the most favourable position to develop both nahualism and healing, together with those born under Itzcuintli, the glyph of the dog, and under *Malinalli*, the climbing plant.

The Two Cycles of Life

Life has two main cycles: the waking and sleep states, which together make up the 'small cycle', and life and death, which form the 'big cycle'.

Every night when we fall asleep our nahual goes to Temictli, the 'land of dreams', and when we die most of us will go to the Mictlan, the 'place of the dead'. These two energy worlds are very similar, they closely border each other and are both located in the North, the direction of death. This is why training while asleep is used as preparation for the 'big movement' of death, because this is how we learn to move with our energy body.

This tradition regards death as a force that permanently accompanies life as its counterpart, and life and death are symbolized by the same essence, *Coatlicue*, which is one of the Earth's epithets: 'the one who wears a skirt made of snakes'. In Mexico, a huge monolith depicts Coatlicue. It was sculpted exclusively at night and portrays the forces that lurk around in the shadow: death and the night, the Moon and the 'unknown'. Beside the skirt, Coatlicue's head is also formed by two snakes facing each other, symbolizing the permanent meeting of life and death; life and death complement each other and are merely separated by one minor factor, namely time.

According to tradition, the force of death is always located to the left of one's energy, constantly waiting for the right moment to come in through the navel and bring about one's biggest transmutation, that is to say the transformation of the living into a dead person, a state that is regarded as another life. This is the reason why the 'men and women of knowledge' would constantly protect their navels: for instance, to prevent death from gaining access, you can place a seed inside it, especially a grain of corn or a black bean, or even a small pebble made of obsidian, kept in place by a red ribbon. This is an extremely simple practice, but it can lengthen your life, thereby granting you enough time to sort out your issues and die without unfinished business. If you have already taken the decision to create your 'energy double', it will give you some extra time to accomplish this supreme achievement towards a great death. Before casting our minds in this direction, however, we must start taking a few steps using the practices that are shown in this book: cleansing the shadow, recovering our discipline and our willpower, beginning to recall our dreams... Future books will be devoted to the various subsequent steps.

Learn how to Die

The Coatlicue monolith summarizes–for those who know how to look, or have already been trained–all the knowledge that the *Mexihcahtzin,* the venerable Mexicas, held on death. Up to now we have discussed how to live and how to dream, whereas now we shall look into how to die, in an attempt to ensure that this takes place in the best possible way.

The ancient Mexica culture was neither self-complacent, nor would it guarantee a return to the Sun or the 'great death' at the end of time to everyone, which is why everyone did their level best to 'blossom' in this life, not knowing whether they might be given a second chance: life revolved around right living and right dreaming, and preparing for a great death.

The Three Types of Death
- **Exiting the body via the liver:
  the death of ordinary human beings**
  As I have already mentioned, the force of death comes in via the navel and expels the ihiyotl, the 'life breath', through the liver: this is how ordinary human beings usually die, if they have not embarked upon the pursuit of their 'blossoming'. As you may recall, the calendar contains a wheel that is composed of twenty glyphs: the first one is Cipactli, the crocodile, or in other words the energy that nourishes us, while the last one is Xochitl, the flower. If we do not manage to 'blossom' in the

Coatlicue graphically portrays the training on how to die. The most common type of death (that involves both navel and liver) is here represented by the skull; a more enlightened type of death (where the body is exited through the heart) is depicted by either a butterfly, which symbolizes the death of women-warriors, or a hummingbird, symbolizing the death of men-warriors; and the head made of snakes represents the energy double that must be developed by an authentic nahual, to allow him or her to die and exit the body via the crown of the head (National Museum of Anthropology of Mexico).

glyph under which we are born, in our next life we will not have any other choice than to be born as humans under the following glyph, and so on and so forth until we reach Xochitl. If, however, we do not achieve it even under this glyph, we will be reborn again under Cipactli, but this time with a different set of numerical data (the solar waves), which will create different conditions for blossoming and attaining enlightenment. It is common knowledge that the wheel is not eternal, as we are endowed with a finite amount of energy with which to complete our journey; if the energy that is available to us runs out before the blossoming takes place, we will proceed directly to the Mictlan, the 'place of the dead', where we will have another opportunity to bring our suffering to an end, as we shall see later.

- **Exiting the body via the heart:
  the death that leads us to the Sun**
  Here death enters via the navel and expels the ihiyotl through the heart, i.e., the location of the teyolia. To bring about such a result we should have 'cleansed' the entire energetic path of the totonalcayo, i.e., the energy points or wheels, which are located between the coccyx and the crown of the head. How do we manage to achieve this type of cleansing? We must heal the 'old winds', both our own and our ancestors', and get rid of all the burdensome causes of our anger and shame, given that we have nothing to forgive, nor to ask forgiveness for; this is because we have not retained other people's energy inside us, nor have we left ours inside them, and this releases us from having to come back. Naturally we will have also cleansed our shadow and fully mastered our dreams.

  Such an accomplishment will cause our name to be listed in the category of 'warriors', and this will mean that a reward is reserved for us. Dying in a lightened state while exiting through the heart enables us to rise up to the Second Heaven and to follow the Sun in its orbit for four years, while continuing to preserve our individuality. Later we will be able to choose whether we want to merge with the Sun and become part of it, living our life from its perspective, or whether we want to return to Earth as a hummingbird (in the case of men), or as a butterfly (in the case of women), those animals that are regarded as evolutionary archetypes, in that they do not possess either a shadow nor a complementary duality. When we therefore notice a particular hummingbird or butterfly, we will know that we are in front of a light warrior, a great master who is returning to Earth where he or she will continue to teach, albeit in a different manner.

- **Exiting the body via the crown of the head: permanent individuality**
  This is the type of death sought by those who want to reach further than the Sun, and do not wish to merge either with its light or with the shadow of the Mictlan, but would rather keep their individuality and therefore be capable of transcending both life and death, as well as light and shadow. This level of achievement requires the perfect mastery of the energy body and its outcome is the eternal journey in the physical and subtle worlds on the part of the Mexihcahtzin, 'the venerable Mexicas', and obviously of the *nahuales*[37] too.

Experiencing this state of merger, namely the return to the unity of the All through a series of specifically related exercises, is part of the training on how to die by exiting through the heart. This state of merger is the goal of most spiritual traditions that currently exist on our planet. Having experienced through perseverance this state while still alive, in the Mexica tradition we can ask ourselves instead whether we really want to abide permanently in the light of the Sun and in this state of unity, or whether we might prefer to go back to our individuality.

For those brave men and women who decide that their destiny ought to be greater than the state of unity, the most difficult part actually comes now, and it requires an even higher level of discipline than that achieved by the warriors: it requires the opening

---

37 Plural form of nahual (translator's note).

of the channel that runs from the heart to the head, namely the creation of an 'energy double' where one can continue to exist freely and on an individual basis, where one is subject exclusively to one's own laws and is able to travel to any universe, including those which at present remain inaccessible to human perception. These are the universes of the *yeyelli*, the 'inorganic' or 'energetic' beings, or of the *pipiltin*, 'beings who manifest in the worlds of matter and of energy', which our world also belongs to.

Other Destinies

Death opens up several possible destinies: children and young people who have not had any sexual experiences will go back to the Second Heaven, to the 'mother-tree' on whose branches they will await their new birth; those who have died either by drowning or struck by lightning will go to Tlalocan, a kind of paradise located in the South, where they will remain at the playful service of Tlaloc, the essence of Water, and their playful games will be perceived by us humans as rain and thunder. All the corpses that were found at the bottom of wells were therefore the outcome of voluntary actions, given that death by drowning would guarantee these people their place in paradise. Unlike popular belief, therefore, these were not examples of human sacrifices.

For the majority of humans, however, the energy that would allow them to return to Earth runs out before they can reach their 'blossoming', and in this case a different type of destiny will open up for them, one final opportunity to achieve, once they are dead, all that they could not manage to bring to fruition while they were still alive. In the Mictlan, the 'place of the dead', they will have four years allocated to them during which they can make up for it, and overcome the challenges of the first eight underworlds with the aim of reaching the ninth, the place of eternal rest. As these four years are spent in the energy worlds, they will last much longer than four years spent in the physical world, yet many will nonetheless use them up before being able to go beyond one single underworld, or when they happen to go through their most challenging underworld; they will then lose their individual essence, which becomes reabsorbed into the shadow, into this undifferentiated energy: such loss of individuality becomes a real torment, as they are stripped of their individual experiences and memories and are made to return to the essence of the being that is held inside the shadow. Nothing will remain of what once was their individual energy: neither memories, nor any traces whatsoever.

As things stand at present, it is very useful to have prior awareness of the various aspects of the Mictlan to gain a full understanding of what we may be able to resolve in this life, and consequently die a great death.

The Mictlan, 'the Place of the Dead'

In the North, under the rule of Yayauhqui Tezcatlipoca and governed by *Mictlantecuhtl* and *Mictlancihuatl,* the lords of the underworlds, lies Mictlan.

Whoever travels there without having 'blossomed' will have to face several trials before reaching the ninth and last underworld, 'the place of eternal rest': these trials are the same as those we have to deal with in life, which means therefore that in death we will have to accomplish what we neglected to do while still alive.

Understanding what happens in the Mictlan is tantamount to understanding what targets we must achieve in life, if we want to 'blossom', so much so that one of my masters refers to it as, "the place reserved for those men who have spent their lives watching football, and for those women who have spent them watching soap operas".

Here follows a presentation of the nine underworlds, or 'worlds below', which make up the Mictlan:

- **Apanahuiayan** means 'crossing the river'.
  According to tradition, at this stage the dead person must cross two rivers, and on arriving at the second will receive the help of a brown-coloured dog.
  These two rivers are a metaphor for the passage from the river of the living to that of the dead without losing consciousness; in other words, death in a state of awareness, with no fear whatsoever, and being aware of entering a new existence.

The most advanced aspect of any dream-related training entails daily visualisations of this underworld, while
maintaining both consciousness and identity as we move
from the river of the tonal, the waking state, to that of the
nahual, or sleep state; this exercise will eventually allow
us to develop control of our energy body, which in turn
will enable us to control our death in a similar way.

If you own a dog, its nahual will play a role that is particularly important in this transition: the Mexica 'men
and women of knowledge' used to own dogs, which they
held in great respect and would look after with great care
because they knew that they would meet them at this stage.

- *Tepetlmonamictia,* 'the meeting of the mountains'.

According to tradition, here we find ourselves in front
of two twin mountains, which are separated by a path.
When the dead person tries to follow this path, these
mountains come close together to block the way, and he
or she could end up spending the whole four years in a
futile attempt to cross them, and being stripped of the
essence of their soul before being able to do so.

The metaphor which originates from this underworld is a
very deep one: the two mountains are both perfectly identical and the mirror image of each other. This explains
why in the ancient Mexica tradition the use of the obsidian mirror was so important: it was used to see beyond
what the simple image would illustrate; the first image
that we perceive is our tonal, but if we look closer we
will see our nahual, which appears in different shapes;
if we look even more closely, we will discover that we
are in the Mictlan and eventually we will realize that we
are dead. The mountains will let through only those who
know themselves in the waking and dream states, as well
as when dead, a form of knowledge that we can achieve
while still alive: we can remove the thick energy and
thanks to the mirror discover who we are; we can face
our darkness with the aim of encountering our luminous
side, and learn not to lose consciousness when we fall
asleep, so as to avoid losing it when we die.

- **Itztepetl,** literally 'the mountain made of obsidian daggers'.

  This underworld too has a very important lesson in store, both for the living and the dead.

  Here the willpower of the warrior is evoked, which spurs him on to walk anywhere, even over the obsidian blades: the daggers in this case symbolize our problems, our weak points, and nowadays we mostly lack the desire to overcome them. To develop the willpower that would allow us to transcend all our limitations, the ancient Toltec tradition (*toltecayotl*) contains some gruelling sacred dance and body control training drills. At this stage we must bear in mind that if we do not develop it while we are still alive, we will end up having to do so once we are dead.

  The dead person, still equipped with an illusory physical body, will have to walk over the daggers' blades, which will cause him or her excruciating pain. Each dagger will represent an unresolved problem, something that he will not have been able to accomplish due to his weak willpower, some unfinished business, and the daggers will not disappear until he has fully resolved everything he had preferred to postpone until later in his life. Sometimes the dead remain trapped at this point, either because of a lack of willpower or fear of pain, and they do not proceed any further along their path: in this way they waste away the four years that are still available to them and all that they will have perceived is a place of infinite sorrow, instead of viewing it as their last available opportunity to be able to forge their will as a spiritual warrior. Eventually nothing will be left of their essence.

- **Paniehecatlacayan,** literally 'the flags blown about by the wind'.

  If we want to understand the lesson of this underworld, we should be familiar with the ancient Mexicas' concept of wind, in that they regarded it as the messenger, or the conduit for everything.

  The 'old winds' are the type of slothfulness that we have

inherited from our ancestors, from our journey and all the experiences of our teyolia, our soul. *Pantli,* 'the flag', is the name of the third of our totonalcayo, an energy point located in the navel. In the Paniehecatlacayan, our 'flag' (our power) is perpetually blown about by the old winds, and therefore we will never distance ourselves from the paths marked out by our ancestors, or from our well-beaten tracks; buffeted along by the old winds we invariably repeat the same old patterns, devoid of any will, of any new movement or change. Overcoming this underworld equates to overcoming all forms of conditioning, all patterns which have been imposed upon us: and we must live through this Sun's transformation now, while we are still alive, otherwise we will have to do it once we are dead, and undergo a much more complex trial: we will have to slow the winds down to bring the flag to a standstill.

- *Itzehecayan,* 'the site of freezing winds'.
Here the winds make us freeze and prevent us from moving forward. Nowadays, this is a very common situation, even while we are still alive: fear and laziness are the forces that keep us frozen and paralyze our ability to act.
Only those who manage to defeat both their fear and laziness have the power to defrost themselves while living. As regards the dead, they should have trained while still alive to understand the way things work in this underworld: as soon as we drop all our fears, the freezing wind disappears and crossing Itzehecayan becomes possible.

- *Temiminaloyan,* 'the place where we are chased by arrows'.
This underworld holds a great lesson in store for us: the warriors that accompany the Sun will start shooting arrows of fire at the dead located further below, who will have to try and avoid them. For both Mexicas and Toltecs the arrow symbolizes direction, while the fire represents dreams: avoiding the fiery arrow, therefore, means avoiding that our direction be dictated by someone else's dreams, and consequently becoming warriors who have the capacity to give direction to their life and their

dreams. If due to laziness or lack of discipline we were to give up exerting control over our dreams, we would never lighten our tonal and this level of slothfulness would end up conditioning our dreams, and as a consequence our lives as well. If we intend to control our dreams, we must practise while we are still alive, so that when we are dead we may be able to transcend this underworld and transform ourselves into arrows, embarking upon whichever direction we may choose.

During the sowing of the name ceremony, those who receive a name shoot an arrow in the direction of the Sun to signify that it is their destiny, and in so doing they identify which direction to follow: this action refers specifically to what I have just explained.

- *Teyollocualoyan*, 'the place where the heart is eaten by wild beasts'.

For the dead person to be able to go beyond Teyollocualoyan, all those 'thick' emotions he could not free himself from in life must now disappear: that is to say, all forms of attachment and anything else which overloads the emotional body. If the dead person cannot let go of these emotions, the wild beasts will carry on devouring his or her heart, thus perpetuating this endless torture.

Often in life we remain attached to specific feelings which we do not want to give up, even though they may cause us a great deal of suffering. The ancient 'men and women of knowledge', however, would cleanse their emotions, because they realized that these have no true existence within the movement. They would rid themselves of the energy of others and retrieve their own, to be free of all emotional ties and thereby follow the path that leads either to the Sun, or to their own individual destiny.

- *Itzmictlanapochaloca*, 'the place where clouds become darker'.

This underworld, the eighth, represents the ultimate ordeal: it is a completely dark place, where the only possibility of salvation lies in having developed to some extent the inner vision that brings light, and in having worked towards bringing one's own cave, one's own darkness under control; this is why the Yayauhqui Tezcatlipoca, the black Tezcatlipoca, is always shown with his eyes blindfolded, to symbolize that the inner knowledge is aware of all the answers and that it will lead us along the right path, once we have managed to tame the shadow.

The dead who manage to transcend all these underworlds will realize all that they had not realized when alive, and will therefore receive some kind of reward: they will reach the 'Place of eternal rest', the ninth underworld.

- *Chiconauhmictlan*, 'the Ninth Underworld'.

  This is the place that is reached only by the most developed beings, after a very long journey. It is also considered the place of eternal peace.

  Some masters say that those who have reached this place may decide to go back to Earth, and then–endowed with all this experience–attempt to become united with the Sun.

How to Help Someone who is Trapped in One of the Underworlds

The breathing exercise that was presented in Chapter 9 contained a movement whereby we would summon our ancestors for the purpose of healing them: this is actually very helpful for them, as it is meant to enable them to go beyond any of the underworlds in which they may find themselves trapped.

Ometeotl!

The Path of Quetzalcoatl, the White Tezcatlipoca

"For many are called, but few are chosen"
(Matthew 22:14)

At last we have reached the path that is reserved for those who have managed to cleanse their cave and to renew themselves and who, having overcome the trials of their individual underworlds, have managed to persevere through discipline until the end result.

This path of recognition of the Sun–symbolized by an eagle– is the path of Quetzalcoatl, which many endeavour to follow, but which only very few succeed in exploring fully.

Quetzalcoatl, the white Tezcatlipoca, is the title conferred upon those who have attained the mastery of a specific type of knowledge, and who, most of all, have managed to rise to and overcome their main challenge, i.e., knowing how to direct their life towards the warrior's great death: this will guide them to either accompany the Sun along its course or to opt for their eternal individuality.

This word comes from the verb *quetza*, which means 'to raise', and from *coatl*, 'serpent', or energy. To put it briefly it means 'the one who has managed to raise his or her energy', or *coatzin*, 'the venerable serpent', so much so that he or she has been transformed into an eagle, or into a *quetzal*, that is to say, the one whose precious energy has blossomed.

As regards their knowledge levels, in ancient times they used to refer to the *quequetzalcoah*, in the plural: there were many types of them, categorised in accordance with the specific sphere of knowledge in which they had been initiated, as we shall see below. Some of them still exist to this day, although they would not refer to themselves in these terms, as a mark of humility.

Quetzalcoatl, the feathered serpent. Teotihuacan, Mexico

Here is the list of Quetzalcoatl's epithets:

- ***Ehecatl Quetzalcoatl***, 'the *Quetzalcoatl* of the Wind', who is familiar with the spirit of the wind, which acts as a messenger, and with whom he has struck an alliance. Given his capacity to communicate and interact with it, he can change the course of events as well as predict the future; furthermore, he can accurately record all the wind's messages, both in the tonal and in the nahual.

  He knows the four winds inside out: *tlauhcopa ehecatl*, 'the yellow wind' from the East, which brings great blessings to humans, coupled with entirely positive replies in the event they have made requests to the wind; *mictlampa ehecatl*, 'the black wind' from the North, the harbinger of death and misfortune, along with negative replies to any of our questions, which however is also the wind of knowledge; *cihuatlampa ehecatl*, 'the red wind' from the West, which restores balance and carries away all curses, besides making all projects thrive; *huitztlampa ehecatl*, 'the white wind' from the South, which removes all thorns from our path and blows away all future obstacles: this is the wind of willpower.

People have lost touch with nature, but in the Sixth Sun the natural laws will regain the upper hand and this contact will be re-established. *Ometeotl!*

We dream of misfortunes before they actually occur,[38] following which we are pre-warned by a gust of wind from the North, which acts as their harbinger. If we do absolutely nothing to alter what is about to happen, it will turn into manifest reality.

This is what usually happens, because people do not remember their dreams, and even if they do, they do not know how to interpret them and, to cap it all, they do not seem to pay any attention to the wind...

All the above seems to apply equally to good things: a dream announces them, following which a pleasant gust of wind comes in from the East.

An Ehecatl Quetzalcoatl knows how to invoke any of these winds to bring about the manifestation of a specific reality. The aim may be to restore the balance of a particular situation, or perhaps eliminate certain difficulties, or maybe simply be as a kind of oracular prediction.

Invoking the wind features amongst the various types of *ehecatl* training that I teach my students, and I can actually recall an occasion when a young woman joined one of my classes in Mexico City in a distressed state: her

---

38 Interpreting dreams using the logic of the tonal is a very common mistake to make: dreaming of death may for instance point to a new beginning, which is why dreams should only be interpreted when the nahual language codes are available to us.

father had recently passed away, and she was eager to know if he was all right, wherever he might be. We put the question to the wind and immediately a gust blew in from the East, the sign of a positive reply. She later told me that from that moment on she felt much calmer and more serene: she was now certain that her father was in a good place.

On another occasion, again in Mexico City, one of my teachers was woken up in the middle of the night by a violent earthquake. He listened to the wind, and noticing that it was not coming from the North, he said to his wife: "Please don't worry and carry on sleeping; this earthquake is not the big one", and he fell asleep again even though the earth continued to shake.

We too can begin to develop this wind listening skill, both in the waking state and in our sleep; we can secure its friendship and its favours, and follow the path of the Quetzalcoatl of the Wind.

- *Tlaloc Quetzalcoatl,* 'the *Quetzalcoatl* of the Water'.
It is often the case that the power of control over the Water is developed by those who have been struck by a bolt of lightning and have managed to survive. The same people may also find themselves endowed with great healing powers. In Mexico they are usually referred to as *granizeros* (*graniz* means hail).

Four are the winds and four are the waters: the benevolent water that makes everything blossom, the water that freezes and destroys, that which causes floods and that 'which does not fully blossom'.

A Tlaloc Quetzalcoatl can scrape the sky vigorously and thereby cause a downpour, and has the ability to hold back the devastating power of the water.

A supreme holder of such powers was Don Lucio, a figure who was much talked and written about in Mexico. It is said that on one occasion a group of Jehovah's Witnesses came to try and convert him to their faith. He asked them: "Do they teach you how to make rain fall in your church?" and when they answered him: "No, only God can make rain fall", he retorted: "I can make rain fall, so if this is not what they teach you in your church, I shall not convert to your faith."

- *Piltzintecuhtli Quetzalcoatl,* 'the child Quetzalcoatl', the one who has painted the creation that was originally dark with colours, the son of the Sun that each morning at dawn ignites life with colour. This is the Quetzalcoatl who holds the knowledge of colours and their effects.

- *Tlahuizcalpantecuhtli Quetzalcoatl,* 'the Quetzalcoatl who is the holder of the knowledge of Venus and her effects', the one who understands her synchronicity with the Moon and consequently the way in which this has an impact on dreams. He can also appear as *Xolotl,* the formless Lord of the knowledge of the shadow: he is the counterpart of Quetzalcoatl, who is the Lord that possesses all useful and precious knowledge, which is why all dream masters belong to this category.

- *Tonatiuh Quetzalcoatl,* 'the Sun's Quetzalcoatl': these were the people who studied the Sun's movements, cycles and effects, to whom we owe most of the materials that make up this book–for instance, the alternation and the duration of those periods called 'Suns'–as well as our interaction with the solar consciousness to overcome the challenges that we face in this life.

- *Xochiquetzalli,* 'the bird that has blossomed'. *Quetzalli* is the female version of *quetzal:* it is the name by which the women who hold the knowledge of all female forces, of the Moon cycles and of all female treatment and therapies are referred to. Xochiquetzalli also symbolizes Mother Earth.

- *Ichpocatzin,* 'the venerable smoking power'. This is the name reserved for medicine women, the holders of the knowledge of Mother Earth and her cycles, and of the secrets of the plants; they use the smoke of copal in their healing practices.

- *Xochipilli Quetzalcoatl,* 'the noble Lord of the flowers', holder of the knowledge of the universe (the flower), Lord and master of life that blossoms and flowers in all its aspects. He is the one who can die in a state of full awareness, exiting the body through either the heart or the crown of the head, and who can either unite himself with the Sun, or maintain his individuality. Becoming a xochipilli means achieving realization in all aspects of life, including poetry, dance and obviously the knowledge of flowers and their power. The most important xochipilli is naturally the one who knows and rules over the 'flower of the universe' (see Figure on page 5), and as such is omniscient: he knows the thirteen heavens, symbolized by the flower's pistils, the four directions, represented by its petals, the nine underworlds, symbolized by the stalk, and the centre of the flower, namely *Tlalticpac*, 'the place where we live'.

The conquest of the four petals or cardinal points is the supreme conquest of existence. Each of them symbolizes a real success story, a challenge that has been successfully met while living on this planet: by conquering the petal of the North, the Quetzalcoatl will receive from this direction the positive customs and wisdom of his ancestors, coupled with the ability to dismantle the destructive slothfulness of the mecatl, his blood lineage. Through the conquest of the petal of the East he will be endowed with both the warriors' courage and discipline and with the Sun's brightness, by means of which he will be able to overcome the challenge posed by his own glyph. When conquering the petal of the West he will obtain the power of life and death over the events of his own life by means of his female counterpart, *Cihuacoatl*, the snake-woman; he will thus receive her healing powers as well as the strength of fertility that can cause the growth of all that is desired. Lastly, through the petal of the South, the location of the Tlalocan, i.e., the home of all emotions, he will be able to temper and dominate his own emotions, and will thus make the flower reach its full completion.

Quetzalcoatl is above all 'he who has blossomed', as we can see from the cover of this book; from there he calls out to you so that you too may blossom by entering one of the most profound traditions on Earth, which is making a comeback at the dawn of the Sixth Sun... *Ometeotl!*

EXERCISE

The Transformation from Tezcatlipoca to Quetzal or Eagle

As previously mentioned, Quetzalcoatl originates from the black Tezcatlipoca, therefore our realization will start by cleansing our shadow, as you have already been told.

One of the images in the codexes portrays Tezcatlipoca blindfolded, sporting the drawing of the jaguar *Ocelotl* on his left leg and the crocodile *Cipactli* on the right one, the serpent *Coatl* along his spine, the lizard *Cuetzpalin* in the genital area, *Huitzilin*, the hummingbird that flies to the left, beside his left ear, and lastly holding the eagle *Cuauhtli* in his right hand.

The animals of power represent the spirit or essence of the animals of the physical world, and they are ritually invoked so that they can transmit their qualities to us, as we can see from the next exercise.

Method

Here too inhale the power of the Sun while counting to 13, and exhale your own shadow while counting to 9.

This process is repeated 13 times.

Now summon the jaguar, the sun of the underworld, and the first animal of power, into your left leg: "*Ocelotl*, xihualhui! Xihualhui!"[39] Allow this energy to flow into your left leg; let it come in and firstly flow downwards, then upwards several times, in so doing cleansing your shadow and finding solutions for your underworlds and your dreams.

When you feel that this has actually taken place, summon the crocodile, the second animal of power, into your right leg: "*Cipactli*, xihualhui! Xihualhui!".

Let this energy flow into your leg, running up and down several times to remove the blockages that have cropped up inside the energy of sustenance and abundance: the right leg is thus freed and it can now receive this rich flow that comes from the Earth, so that it can manifest in your life.

---

39 Pronounced: "shewalwe", translator's note.

When you feel that this has actually happened, summon the lizard, or the third animal of power, to your genital area: "*Cuetzpalin*, xihualhui! Xihualhui!" and feel that its energy is reaching this part of your body, where it cleanses your sexual energy and removes all traces of negativity that you might have created with it during the course of your life.

When you feel that this has happened, summon the venerable serpent *Coatzin* so that it enters via your coccyx (an area called *colotl* in Nahuatl): "*Coatzin*, xihualhui! Xihualhui!"

- In the *colotl* the serpent's energy cleanses the old winds, before starting to rise.
- In the genital area (a spot called *ihuitl*) it removes everything that prevents it from rising upwards.
- In the navel (the area called *pantli*) it purifies the trapped energy that prevents you from clearing up the glyph under which you were born.
- In the chest area (*xochitl*, 'the flower') it heals anything that impedes blossoming.
- In the throat (*topilli*) it heals the speech energy, restoring power to your speech.
- In the forehead (*chalchiuhuitl*, i.e., 'jade') you enter the precious essence of your own being in order to create.
- Once it has reached the crown of your head (*tecpatl*) the serpent cleanses the Tezcatlipoca tonatiuh, your sun of destruction in its entirety.
- Now visualize the transformation of the serpent, which is now growing feathers; the feathered serpent transforms into a hummingbird, which leaves through your left ear.

Now summon the spirit of the hummingbird: "*Huitzilin*, xihualhui! Xihualhui!" and request that its powers bestow upon you both willpower and the gift of prophecy, as well as the power of control over your dreams. Let this energy flow through your right arm: once it has reached your hand, let it transform itself into an eagle.

Now summon the spirit of the eagle: "*Cuauhtli*, xihualhui! Xihualhui!" The arrival of this energy transmits to you the spiritual flight, the knowledge of Quetzalcoatl. Now let the eagle in your hand take off.

Let it fly higher than the Moon, and in so doing dismantle its prison. Your own energy, in the shape of the eagle, rises straight up to the Sun and penetrates it. Allow the entire solar consciousness to come into you.

Once you have received enough energy, join your palms together and state your intention: "From the shadow of my Tezcatlipoca may the light of my Quetzalcoatl be created. *Ometeotl.*"

Sergio Ocelocoyotl, Italy, June 2011

All terms contained in this glossary come from the Nahuatl language unless otherwise indicated.

Amomati: 'the empty mind' state, also called *moyocoyani.*

Anáhuac: 'in between the waters', the Nahuatl name of the entire land that stretches from Alaska down to Nicaragua.

Atl: the Water element.

Atlacahualo: the sub-cycle between 12 and 31 March, or 'what the waters left behind'.

Atonatiuh: the 'Sun of Water', the Fourth Sun.

Camaztli: 'the renewal hunter by means of the breath', one of the epithets of *Xipe Totec.*

Carrizo: a type of Mexican bamboo characterized by an inner cavity.

Ce, or **cen**: one, unity.

Ce Acatl Topiltzin Quetzalcoatl: the last Toltec ruler, born in AD 947 and disappeared in AD 999, traditionally regarded as the supreme achiever of the *Quetzalcoatl* state.

Ce ilhuicatl: 'the First Heaven'. The name of this heaven is *Metztli ilhuicatl*, 'the sky of the Moon', where Moon and clouds move about.

Cehonomeyohcan: the name of the Thirteenth Heaven.

Centeotl: a term made up of *cen*, 'unity', and *teotl*, 'energy', which refers to the unique creative energy that carries in itself the original essence of all that exists, which is not created, is self-invented and cannot be destroyed by anything. This is the generating principle which is also defined as 'what gives life, measure and movement to the creation'.

Centli: from *ce*, or *cen*: 'the *centli* corn' is the creative spirit expressing itself in the corn.

Chac mool *(Mayan)*: literally 'rain bowl'. This is the name in the Mayan language of the statues built to show how to perform specific exercises.

Chalchiuhtotolin: literally 'the jade turkey', one of the epithets of the black Tezcatlipoca.

Chalchiuhuitl: *literally* 'jade', the name of an energy point located on the forehead.

Chicahuaztli: 'the one who leaves his strength inside the Earth for her renewal', one of the epithets of *Xipe Totec*.

Chicnahui: 'nine': this comes from *chic*, 'power', *ce*, 'unity', and *nahui*, 'Mother Earth's order'.

Chicnahui ilhuicatl: 'the Ninth Heaven'. The name of this heaven is *Texouhqui ilhuicatl*, 'the deep blue sky of the cycles'.

Chicnauhmictlan: the 'underworlds'.

Chicoacen: this comes from the roots *chic*, 'power', *cóatl*, 'snake' (which equates to 'energy') and *cen*, 'unity'.

Chicoacen ilhuicatl: 'the Sixth Heaven'. The name of this heaven is *Omeyocan*, 'the place of second duality'.

Chicome: this comes from the roots *chic*, 'power' (where the *c* stands for -*ce* or *cen*, 'unity') and *ome*, 'duality'. Its meaning is 'the power of reunited duality'.

Chicome ilhuicatl: 'the Seventh Heaven'. The name of this heaven is *Iztac Ilhuicatl*, 'the white sky of the Spirit of the Moon'.

Chicomoztoc: 'the cave of power'; according to the oral tradition, on an individual level the 'cave' is our inner dimension, where the shadow takes root. The doors through which it is possible to go back up to the light are the seven energy points called *totonalcayo*.

Chicuey: 'eight'. This comes from the roots *chic*, 'power', *ce*, 'unity' and *onyei*, 'blood flow'.

Chicuey ilhuicatl: 'the Eight Heaven'. The name of this heaven is

Coztic ilhuicatl, 'the golden sky of the Spirit of the Sun'.

Chimal: the shield.

Chitontiliztli: 'the power of the dance'.

Chitontiquiza: literally the 'power of the dance that enables the rise to the sacred level'.

Cihuatlampa: west, the direction of fertility; the residence of female warriors.

Cincalco ilhuicatl: 'the sky of the stars', the name of the Fifth Heaven.

Cipacnahualli: the 'language of the unknown', the symbolic language of dreams.

Cipactli: the crocodile.

Cipactonalli: the numeric or mathematical language of 'what is known', which is still utilized by Nahuatl-speaking people for counting purposes, and which for the mystics represents the explanation of how the entire illusion of the physical universe originates from the initial energy. The language of the waking state. The Nahuatl language, that is sacred because its onomatopoeic words still preserve the authentic vibration of what they represent, in addition to the initiation meaning of the *tlahtolli*.

Citlalli popocas: literally 'smoking stars': the comets.

Coatl: the snake.

Coatlicue: one of the Earth's epithets: 'the one who wears a skirt made of snakes'.

Coatzin: the 'venerable sexual energy' that is symbolized by a snake.

Códices *(Spanish)*: the Scriptures.

Colotl: energy point located in the coccyx.

Copal: an aromatic resin used as offering.

Coyolxauhqui: the Moon, daughter of *Tonantzin Coatlicue*.

Coztic ilhuicatl: 'the golden sky of the Spirit of the Sun'. This is the name of the Eighth Heaven.

Cuauhtémoc: the last great tlahtoani, who made a speech in front of the entire Mexica population, which represents his bequest to posterity and is famously known as *Cuauhtémoc's Legacy.*

Cuauhtlahteotl: 'the family tree', one of the epithets of *Huitzilopochtli.*

Cuauhxicalli: the Toltec-Mexica calendar.

Cuicacalli: buildings for dancing, singing and the arts.

Ehecatl: the Wind element.

Ehecatonatiuh: the 'Sun of the Wind', the Second Sun.

Ensoñación (Spanish): dreaming while awake state.

Ensueño (Spanish): dreaming while awake state.

Huehuetl: a drum that usually follows certain patterns, rhythms and sequences based upon the number four, which symbolize the pulsations of the Earth.

Hueyac tlacah: literally the 'big beings of the Earth', or the giants.

Huitzilin: the hummingbird.

Huitzilopochtli: this means several things: it is the 'hummingbird that flies to the left', the principal deity of the Mexicas; it is the rising Sun; it is equally the energy that rules the Southern direction in the waking state world and which removes all thorny obstacles from the path, bestows the strength to persevere and bring all projects to fruition; it is also the warrior who is equipped with both discipline and willpower, and it is the 'blue *Tezcatlipoca*'.

Huitztlampa: South, the direction of the Hummingbird, which represents the determination to overcome all difficulties, as well as the universe of lucid dreaming. The South is also the direction of *Tlalocan*, the Heaven of the Four Waters.

Huitztli: 'thorn'.

Ihiyotl: the 'essence' or 'divine breath', the life force that comes from the subtle worlds and keeps matter alive; the subtle body that is anchored in the liver.

Ihuicatlmatini: 'sage of the heavens'.

Ihuitl: energy point located in the genital area.

Ixcuinan: one of the female epithets of *Tezcatlipoca*, whose meaning is 'the mother who protects the face'.

Ixnextli: one of the female epithets of *Tezcatlipoca*, which literally means 'she whose head is covered in ash'.

Ixquimilli: 'the one who fasts and covers his eyes', one of the epithets, or names, of the black *Tezcatlipoca*.

Itzcuintli: the Dog.

Iztac Ilhuicatl: 'the white sky of the Spirit of the Moon', the name of the Seventh Heaven.

Iztactonatiuh: 'the white Sun', the Sixth Sun.

Iztlacoliuhqui: 'where the obsidian daggers clash', a place in the Eighth Heaven.

Itztlapaltotec: 'the Lord of the red obsidian', one of the epithets of *Xipe Totec*.

Kukulcan (Mayan): this name indicates the same symbol of light and knowledge as *Quetzalcoatl*.

Llorona (Spanish): the 'wailing one'.

Mah toteotahtzin mitsmopieli: 'the tale of our Venerable Land'.

Mahcuilli: 'five'. This comes from *maitli*, 'the hand' and *cuilli*, 'worm' (but also 'fingertips').

Mahcuilli ilhuicatl: 'the Fifth Heaven'. The name of this heaven is *Ollin Ilhuicatl*, 'sky in motion'.

Mahtlactli: 'ten'. This comes from *maitli*, 'hand' and *tlactli*, 'back': 'the back of the hand', as when we show the palm of our hand with its five fingers, and then we turn it to show its back and the 'other' five fingers, which are the complementary aspect of the previous ones.

Mahtlactli ilhuicatl: 'the Tenth Heaven'. The name of this heaven is *Tlatlauhqui ilhuicatl*, 'the deep red sky of wisdom'.

Mahtlactli omome: 'twelve'. *Omome* means 'and two' and includes *ome* which means 'two' and 'complementarity'.

Mahtlactli omome ilhuicatl: 'the Twelfth Heaven'.

Mahtlactli once: 'eleven'. This comes from *mahtlactli*, 'back of the hand', *on*, 'and', and *ce*, 'one'. The name of this heaven is *Teteocan*, 'where the gods abide'.

Mahtlactli onyei: 'thirteen'. *Onyei* means 'and three'.

Mahtlactli onyei ilhuicatl: 'the Thirteenth Heaven'. The name of this heaven is *Cehonomeyohcan.*

Malinalli: a climbing plant.

Mecatl: 'the blood lineage', i.e. the family lineage.

Metztli: the Moon, another female name for the black *Tezcatlipoca.*

Metztli ilhuicatl: 'the sky of the Moon', where Moon and clouds move about, is the name of the First Heaven.

Mexihcah: the Mexicas; literally, the 'location of the navel of the Moon'.

Mexihcahtzin: 'the venerable *Mexihcah*' (or *Mexica*), postures which are synchronized with a specific number of breaths.

Mexihcahyotl: the pre-Hispanic tradition of Mexico, which corresponds to Aztecs and Toltecs.

Mictlampa: North, the direction of death, where our ancestors and the world of dreaming reside.

Mictlan: the 'place of the dead ones'.

Mictlanmatini: 'sage of the underworlds'.

Miquiztli: 'death'.

Mixcoatl: 'the cloudy snake' of the Milky Way, also called 'the star and dawn hunter'. *Quetzalcoatl*'s father. One of the epithets of *Xipe Totec.*

Monenequi: one of the black *Tezcatlipoca*'s epithets, literally meaning 'the one who does what he/she likes, according to his/her own will'.

Moquehqueloa: one of the black *Tezcatlipoca*'s epithets, literally meaning 'the one who makes a mockery of us'.

Moyocoyacatzin a yac oquiyocox: one of the black *Tezcatlipoca*'s epithets, meaning 'Nobody formed him, nobody created him, he made himself, of his own will'.

Moyocoyani: the prime essence of a being; our potential; our individual component of *centeotl.* One of the epithets of the black Tezcatlipoca.

Nahual: it comes from a Nahuatl root formed by *nehuatl,* 'I', and by *ni ye,* 'am', and therefore it means 'who I really am'; it also comes from the word *nahualli,* meaning 'what can be extended'.

A cold energy, which moves in circular movements and resides in the navel area outside the physical body during the waking state, whereas when we fall asleep it moves to occupy the location of the *tonal* around the head, leading our perception to all kinds of subtle worlds. The *nahual* is the governing energy during the sleep state, as well as the term used to refer to whoever develops the power of this energy: therefore the *nahuales* or *nahualli* are the 'sages who united sleep and wake'. *Nahual* is the term indicating the essences, or energies, of everything that lives in both the physical and subtle universes; it also means a powerful animal that appears in lucid dreams to give instructions.

Nahui: 'four'; this comes from *nantli*, 'mother' and *hui*, 'order': 'the order of the mother', which obviously refers to Mother Earth.

Nahui ilhuicatl: 'the Fourth Heaven'. The name of this heaven is *Cincalco ilhuicatl*, 'the sky of the stars'.

Nahui ollin: the four movements.

Necoc yaotl: 'the mutual enemy', one of the epithets of the black *Tezcatlipoca*.

Nemontemis: four days governed by a fifth between 7 and 11 March, i.e. before the New Year, when it is possible to exert influence over a whole year.

Nezahualpilli: 'the one who fasts and has overcome all his weaknesses', one of the epithets of the black *Tezcatliopoca*.

Nextli: 'the ash', one of the epithets of the shadow.

Nopal: a cactus.

Ocelocoyotl: coyote jaguar.

Ocelotonatiuh: the 'Sun of the Jaguar', the First Sun.

Ohmaxal: see *Onmaxal*.

Ohometeotl (onometeotl or *even ohomeyocan)*: by adding the syllable *oh* the prayer *ometeotl* will be much deeper and more effective, and will reach the Twelfth Heaven.

Ohonomeyocan: 'the place of complementary duality', the name of the Twelfth Heaven.

Ollin: the movement.

Ollin Ilhuicatl: 'sky in motion', the name of the Fifth Heaven.

Ollintonatiuh: the 'Sun of Movement', the Fifth Sun.

Ome: 'two'; this comes from the Nahuatl *omitl*, i.e. 'bone'. The original energy divides itself into two so as to create everything, and as far as we humans are concerned, it is imprinted in our bones even before we come into this world.

Ome ilhuicatl: 'the Second Heaven'. The name of this heaven is *Tonatiuh ilhuicatl*, 'the sky of the Sun'.

Omecíhuatl: 'lady of Duality' (literally: Mrs Two).

Ometecuhtli: 'lord of Duality' (literally: Mr Two).

Ometeotl: from *ome* and *teotl* comes this traditional expression, which means 'may this become real' or, more literally, 'the two energies [may combine to create]'. It also means 'the union of the energy heavens and of the physical world'. This term means that the dualistic energy becomes united in accordance with a very precise order, before descending from the subtle worlds down to the physical one, to the *Tlalticpac*, the Earth, the place where we live. *Ometeotl* is a word of power that moves the thirteen heavens, the nine underworlds and the four directions of our intermediate world, meaning the entire flower that symbolizes the universe.

Omeyocan: 'the place of the second duality', the name of the Sixth Heaven; it has two roots: *ome*, 'two', and *yei*, 'three'.

Onmaxal: the 'cosmic cross', or 'dynamic cross'; the convergence of all subtle forces which keep creating on a continuous basis, thus giving birth to each instant.

Ontlaixco: one part of the Twelfth Heaven is the 'lofty thinking', the creative original thinking divided into a feminine and a masculine aspect, namely into 'father-thought' and 'mother-thought', which are depicted by two parallel lines running respectively from East to West and from West to East.

Ozomahtli: the Monkey.

Oztoteotl: 'the Lord of the caves', one of the epithets of the black *Tezcatlipoca*.

Painalli: literally 'the one who runs fast', a synonym of 'movement'. One of the epithets of *Huitzilopochtli*.

Pantli: literally 'the flag', the name of the third of our totonalcayo, an energy point located in the navel.

Pelota (Spanish): the game of *pelota*, played with a kind of rubber ball, was actually not a game at all: it was a form of training for the best warriors.

Pipiltin: beings who manifest in the worlds of matter and of energy; it also means 'the noble ones'.

Quequetzalcoah: plural of *Quetzalcoatl*.

Quetzalcoatl: *Quetzal* is a sacred bird, but this word equally derives from the verb *quetza*, or 'elevate oneself'; a level of knowledge that can be reached on an individual basis following a personal training process; the 'white *Tezcatlipoca*'.

Quetzalcoatl tonatiuh: the Sun that is the source of life, heat and knowledge.

Quiahtonatiuh: the 'Sun of the Rain of Fire', the Third Sun.

Quincunce: a calendar figure symbolizing the Venus-Moon cycle.

Tecpatl: the obsidian dagger, or flint knife symbolizing the power of the Sun; also the name of an energy point located on the crown of the head.

Telpochtli: 'the one who falls and makes us fall over weaknesses', one of the epithets of the black *Tezcatlipoca*.

Temazcal: from *temaz*, 'steam' and *calli*, 'house'; the Mexica tradition's 'sweat lodge', shaped like an igloo.

Temictli: 'the land of dreams'; the 'uncontrolled dreaming' from which we can have access to the *temixoch*.

Temixoch: the 'blossoming of dreams', the 'controlled and lucid dreaming of a master' who possesses the capacity to sow dreams and make them 'blossom'.

Tenochtitlan: ancient name of Mexico City.

Teocalli: the temples.

Teotl: the energy.

Tepeyolohtli: 'the Lord of the heart of mountains', one of the epithets of the black *Tezcatlipoca*.

Tepeyolotl: 'guardian of the mountain'.

Tepochcalli: *pelota* courts.

Teteocan: 'where the gods abide', the name of the Eleventh Heaven.

Tetzahuitl: 'the amazing', one of the epithets of *Huitzilopochtli*.

Texouhqui ilhuicatl: 'The deep blue sky of the cycles': this is the name of the Ninth Heaven.

Texouhqui Tezcatlipoca: 'the blue *Tezcatlipoca*', also known as *Huitzilopochtli*.

Teyolia: 'the energy around the heart'.

Teyocoyani: 'the one who invents people'.

Tezcatlipoca: from *tezcatl*, 'mirror', and *poca*, 'smoke', thus meaning 'smoking mirror', i.e. the creator of matter and of what cannot be seen clearly.

Tezcatlipoca tonatiuh: the Sun of destruction', one of the epithets of the black *Tezcatlipoca*.

Tezcatzoncatl: 'the group of those who know the mirror'; those who practise a certain kind of breathing.

Thlauhcopa: east, the direction of the Sun, of the willpower of male warriors, and of knowledge.

Tianquiztli ilhuicatl or *Tlahuizcalpantecuhtli ilhuicatl*: 'the sky of the Pleiades and the great star Venus', the name of the Third Heaven.

Titlacahuan: 'the other [I] of the heart', one of the epithets of the black *Tezcatlipoca*.

Tlahtoani: 'the bearer of the word' who communicated the decisions taken by the members of the three councils ruling the weakest of all Aztec groups; he was their social and spiritual leader.

Tlahtolli: the movement that spreads from the subtle worlds to the physical world by means of a mathematical order; the order of creation.

Tlalli: the Earth element.

Tlaloc: the essence or energy of Water.

Tlalocan: the Heaven of the Four Waters.

Tlalticpac: 'the place where we live'; the intermediate world in which we live, in between the heavens and the underworlds, which corresponds to the centre of the flower.

Tlamacazqui: 'he who looks after the essences' (or energies).

Tlamatinime: 'the wise men'.

Tlahnequi: one of the black *Tezcatlipoca*'s epithets, meaning 'the one who has sexual desires'.

Tlatlauhqui: 'what shines and becomes red'.

Tlatlauhqui ilhuicatl: 'the deep red sky of wisdom', the name of the Tenth Heaven.

Tlatlauhqui Tezcatlipoca: 'the red *Tezcatlipoca*', known as *Xipe Totec*.

Tletl: the Fire element.

Tloqueh in Nahuaqueh: it is the energy, or essence, of the inside and of intimate proximity, represented by a hand.

Tollán: Tula, the Toltec capital.

Tonacayo: the physical body.

Tonal: the 'heat'; the waking state; the energy that is located around the head in the waking state.

Tonalli: the light of the day.

Tonantzin: 'our venerable Mother'.

Tonantzin Cuatlicue: the ancient Mother Earth of Mexico City; the mother of *Huitzilopochtli*.

Tonatiuh: the sun.

Tonatiuh ilhuicatl: 'the sky of the Sun', the name of the Second Heaven.

Topilli: energy point located in the throat.

Totolin: 'the turkey'.

Totonalcayo: 'the seven doors of *chicomoztoc*, the cave of power'; these 'doors' are energy points located in the body, and more specifically in the coccyx, the genital area, navel, chest, throat, forehead, and on the crown of the head.

Tzolkin (Mayan): the Mayan calendar.

Tzontemoc: 'the solar fire'.

Xipe Totec: 'our Lord of sloughing', 'the one who sheds his skin', is the third force that supports the universe, 'the red *Tezcatlipoca*', 'the essence of renewal', or of fertility.

Xiuhcóatl: 'the fire snake', which governs renewal in dreams; one of the epithets of *Xipe Totec*.

Xochiquetzalli: complementary aspect of *Xipe Totec*, a young woman who symbolizes the Earth.

Xochitl: 'the flower', an energy point located in the chest area.

Yaotl: 'the enemy', one of the epithets of the black *Tezcatlipoca*.

Yayauhqui Tezcatlipoca: 'the black *Tezcatlipoca*'.

Yei: 'three'; this comes from the word *yeztli*, which means 'blood'. For our ancestors, 'blood' meant the energy (*teotl*) of the universe in the subtle worlds.

Yei ilhuicatl: 'the Third Heaven'. The name of this heaven is *Tianquiztli ilhuicatl* or *Tlahuizcalpantecuhtli ilhuicatl*, 'the sky of the Pleiades and the great star Venus'.

Yeyelli: 'the 'inorganic' or 'energetic' beings.

Yocoya: one of the black *Tezcatlipoca*'s epithets; the idea that the individual being's essence holds about itself.

Yohualli: the darkness of the night.

The richness of this tradition has given rise to the numerous seminars that Sergio Magaña conducts all over the world. It is also possible to take part in some study and practice with Sergio in Mexico, where he lives; some of his masters may also be present and offer their contribution to these events.

For all related information, please visit the Author's website at:

www.sergiomagana.com

or his Facebook page:

https://www.facebook.com/SergioMaganaOcelocoyotl

Alternatively, please write directly to his Institute in Mexico City, at the following address: Centro Energético Integral, Durango 73 – Colonia Roma, Mexico City, Mexico – Tel: (+52) 55141775 or (+52) 55141730.

The seminars

The seminars may be given different titles in different countries and may be subject to slight content alterations to cater for local needs and requirements. Generally, however, the subjects covered are as follows:

Traditional healing

The ancient Toltec-Mexica tradition provides several forms of therapy, some of which will be explored in this seminar. It is however necessary to remind participants that this is an opportunity for study and practice, and it is not therefore intended to be a substitute for any medical treatment that the participants may already be receiving.

The seminar will cover the explanation of those breathing exercises that allow tuning into the rhythm of the universe, and whose movements are described in the sacred calendar. This relates to the 'cleansing of the shadow', a topic which is discussed at length in this book, and which can result in some amazing improvements at the level of personality.

The 'chasing the energy' technique will be taught as well: this will allow practitioners to strengthen their own energy, thereby restoring both health and wellbeing.

The sowing of dreams

The ancient Mexica tradition became specialized in the *nahual*, the dream universe. This seminar will explain its hidden language, and we will learn how to remember and interpret our dreams, with the aim of eliminating all destructive ones.

The main practice taught in this seminar, however, will be the 'sowing of dreams', which makes use of some breathing techniques that allow us to enter into a state of consciousness called 'dreaming while awake', from which we can sow our dreams, thereby creating a different type of reality in the tonal, the physical world.

We will learn how to 'drop or leave behind' all our problems in the world of dreams, and consequently wake up without them. We will discover how to identify ways in which the various types of dullness and lethargy manifest in our dreams, so as to develop a defence mechanism so that the part of us that is asleep can wake us up each time this type of presence is identified. We will be taught the traditional techniques of how to induce and identify both dreams of a prophetic nature and those dreams from which we can extract hidden information, which the ancient cultures consigned to the state of sleep.

The obsidian mirror

This is the mirror from which the term Tezcatlipoca–which means 'smoking mirror', or what cannot be seen clearly–derives; this represents the main traditional tool with which to access the subtle energy worlds in the waking state. We will explore the traditional techniques that were employed to become familiar with one's own 'shadow' by observing its various reflections on the mirror. We will also learn how to use this mirror to acquire new skills and to meet our ancestors in the reflections–thereby giving them some healing–and to create our reality, which we can then use as a source of oracular prediction.

Creating reality

We will explore the four Tezcatlipocas, the forces that sustain the universe, through which we will learn how to sow in *Tonantzin*, Mother Earth, all that we wish to manifest. Based upon the mathematical order of the physical universe and the knowledge of the thirteen heavens, we will learn how to sow our intentions in the mind of the universe, then in our bones and in our blood and lastly into the earth; we will acquire the skill of bringing these intentions to fruition and the ability to overcome our ancestral blockages, so as to be able to 'coagulate' all that we aspire for within this reality. We will learn how to become creators instead of remaining spectators, how to create instead of being created.

Sleep, dreams and death:
training for an enlightened death in the state of awareness,
according to the ancient Toltec-Mexica wisdom

We will be introduced to the descriptions of these states in accordance with the tradition, as well as to the various types of death that correspond to our level of spiritual development. We will learn how to make use of the dream state to overcome the challenges in our life and to complete any unfinished business, so that we can die 'in a state of lightness'; and we will be taught which exercises to do when falling asleep and while dreaming, i.e., the traditional training for dying in the state of awareness.

Have you enjoyed this book?

A number of interviews with this Author with English translation are available on these websites:

- *2012-2021: the Dawn of the Sixth Sun* (http://www.blossomingbooks.com/en/books/2012-2021thedawn.html)

- Amrita Panel Discussions: *What's going to happen in 2012? And after?* (http://multimedia.amrita-edizioni.com/Amrita/Tavole_Rotonde.html)

We have more titles in the pipeline... Watch this space!

www.blossomingbooks.com